Street-Level Leadership

Street-Level Leadership

Discretion and Legitimacy in
Front-Line Public Service

Janet Coble Vinzant
Lane Crothers

GEORGETOWN UNIVERSITY PRESS / WASHINGTON, D.C.

Georgetown University Press, Washington, D.C.   20007
© 1998 by Georgetown University Press. All rights reserved.
Printed in the United States of America.
10 9 8 7 6 5 4 3 2 1 1998
THIS VOLUME IS PRINTED ON ACID-FREE OFFSET BOOKPAPER.

Library of Congress Cataloging-in-Publication Data

Vinzant, Janet Coble.
    Street-level leadership : discretion and legitimacy in front-line
public service / Janet Coble Vinzant, Lane Crothers.
        p.   cm.
    Includes index.
    1. Social workers.   2. Human services personnel.   3. Leadership.
I. Crothers, Lane.   II. Title.
HV40.V56   1998
361'.0068'4—dc21
ISBN 0-87840-704-9 (cloth). — ISBN 0-87840-705-7 (paper)
                                                        98-4477

Contents

Preface   ix

INTRODUCTION   ix

STREET-LEVEL PUBLIC SERVANTS IN ACTION   x

    Case #1   x

    Case #2   xi

    Case #3   xii

    Case #4   xiii

UNDERSTANDING AND EVALUATING THE WORK OF
    FRONTLINE PUBLIC SERVANTS: COMPETING VISIONS   xiv

PLAN OF THE BOOK   xviii

Acknowledgments   xix

1

The Context of Street-Level Public Service   1

INTRODUCTION   2

CORE IDEAS AND ASSUMPTIONS   6

WHAT STREET-LEVEL PUBLIC SERVANTS DO AND WHY IT MATTERS   9

    Mapping the Environment of Contemporary Street-Level
        Public Service   11

    Complexity in Action   17

    Influence, Governance, and Street-Level Public Servants   19

METHODOLOGY AND APPROACH   19

    Genesis   21

    Concept Development and Refinement   22

    The Problems of Participant Observation   24

    The Cases: Agencies and Communities   28

    Shifts and Workers   30

2
Discretion and Legitimacy in Frontline Public Service 32

INTRODUCTION   35
DISCRETION AND LEGITIMACY   35
    The Nature of Discretion   36
    Sources of Discretion in Street-Level Public Service   40
    The Changing Nature and Scope of Discretion   42
    Evaluating the Exercise of Discretion   47
    The Nature of Legitimacy   48
EXISTING MODELS OF PUBLIC SERVICE   54
    Model 1: The Bureaucrat   54
    Model 2: Implementers and Policy Makers   56
    Model 3: The Power Wielder   58
    Model 4: The Professional   59
    Model 5: The Problem Solver   61
    Model 6: The Political Actor   64
DISCRETION, LEGITIMACY, AND EXISTING MODELS OF STREET-LEVEL PUBLIC
    SERVICE: AN ASSESSMENT   66

3
A Model of Street-Level Leadership 68

INTRODUCTION   71
WHY LEADERSHIP?   72
LEADERSHIP AND POWER IN THE CONTEXT OF
    STREET-LEVEL PUBLIC SERVICE   74
    Trait Theories of Leadership   74
    Leadership as Behavior   77
    Situational Approaches to Leadership   79
    Power and the Practice of Leadership   83
    Leadership and the Legitimation of Power   86
UNDERSTANDING STREET-LEVEL PUBLIC SERVANTS AS LEADERS   89
A MODEL OF STREET-LEVEL LEADERSHIP   91

4
Leadership on the Street 95

INTRODUCTION   97
QUADRANT 1: ADMINISTRATIVE PROCEDURE   98
QUADRANT 2: SITUATIONAL LEADERSHIP   101
QUADRANT 3: TRANSFORMATIONAL LEADERSHIP   112

QUADRANT 4: TRANSFORMATIONAL AND
        SITUATIONAL LEADERSHIP   122
"FAILURE" AND LEADERSHIP ON THE STREET   130
CONCLUSION   136

5

Conclusions and Implications   137

INTRODUCTION   141
THE POWER OF THEORIZING   142
IMPLICATIONS OF THE STREET-LEVEL LEADERSHIP MODEL   144
    Street-Level Leadership and the Worker   144
    Street-Level Leadership and Public Organizations   148
    Street-Level Leadership and Governance   149
CREATING STREET-LEVEL LEADERSHIP   152
    Changing Workers   152
    Changing Organizations   154
    Changing Governance   159
THE LIMITATIONS OF STREET-LEVEL LEADERSHIP   161
CONCLUSION   163

Appendix   165

References   171

Index   181

Preface

INTRODUCTION

What is it like to be a street-level public servant? Although there are probably as many answers to that question as there are public servants, there seems to be at least one area of agreement: it can be a very difficult job. Frontline public servants must deal with some of the most persistent and troubling problems in society. They may be called upon to quell a violent crowd, determine when and how to reunite a troubled family, teach an emotionally troubled youth to read, or help an elderly person cope with increasing infirmity. They may be expected to make neighborhoods safe, stop child abuse, cure illiteracy, curb gang activity, reduce dependence, or stop drunk driving. In the course of a single day, they may function as a counselor, an enforcer, a teacher, a facilitator, an analyst, a coach, an investigator, an ombudsman, and a manager.

Such tasks are difficult to accomplish under the best of conditions. Unfortunately, public servants rarely, if ever, do their jobs under ideal circumstances. Instead, they must face these challenges while coping with conflicting expectations, confusing dictates, a critical public, and limited resources. Consider, for example, the following real situations. These cases, like many of those faced by street-level public servants, involve substantial amounts of worker discretion in balancing competing expectations, values, and rules. They also demonstrate the multiple standards by which the actions of frontline public servants can be evaluated. In doing so, they point to the central purpose of this book—to articulate a new model of frontline public service that provides a framework for understanding what street-level public servants do, how they do it, and how the appropriateness and legitimacy of their choices can be evaluated.

STREET-LEVEL PUBLIC SERVANTS IN ACTION

Case #1

Two police officers were dispatched to investigate a report that a car was stalled in the middle of an intersection. When they arrived, the officers found the car in the middle of a four-way stop with a woman passed out at the wheel. After awakening her, the officers asked her to get out of the car and then began their investigation of the incident.

In talking with the woman, the officers learned several things. First, they determined that she was probably intoxicated—she admitted she had been drinking. They also found out that she was only about a block away from her home. Finally, she told them (at which point they recognized her and remembered) that the week before she had witnessed the murder of two family members, a tragedy that had been widely covered by the local media.

During this conversation, the woman was verbally belligerent, but was physically passive. While she clearly did not want to answer the officers' questions and repeatedly insisted that she ought to be allowed to go to her nearby home, she was generally deferential to the officers. Similarly, the officers were verbally firm with her and only restrained her when she attempted to walk out into the street during the interview.

As the investigation progressed, a third officer arrived on the scene. This officer had not been dispatched to the call, but served in a special unit focusing on driving while intoxicated and chose to come. As was his authority according to department rules, he took over the investigation of the incident as soon as he arrived on the scene. The two officers originally dispatched to the call stood aside and simply helped to prevent the woman from leaving the scene.

Less than five minutes after arriving, and after a brief interview with the woman, the third officer made the decision to arrest her for driving while intoxicated. In response, she became both physically and verbally aggressive. She called the officers various names, screamed that she should not be treated this way, threatened the officers with lawsuits if they arrested her, and struggled to get her wrists out of the officers' hands as they attempted to put her in handcuffs. Further, it took both of the officers originally dispatched to the call to get her into the patrol car. She kicked and struggled when the door was opened, so one of the officers had to go to the other side of the car and pull her in across the seat.

Once inside the vehicle, the woman began crying, got angry, and, lying on her back, began kicking the windows in an apparent attempt to break them. The officers warned her to stop. When she continued, they pulled her out of the car, tied her ankles together and her wrists behind her back, put her back in the vehicle, drove her downtown to the jail, and then carried her into the jail still tied. Only when they got to the jail did they release her feet. As soon as they were free, she kicked the wall violently. The officers then filled out the necessary paperwork and left her in the custody of the jailers.

Case #2

An officer was dispatched to a motel in response to a report that an abusive woman was refusing to leave the premises. He called for backup when he was unable to resolve the incident alone. Two officers, including the one with whom the observer was riding, responded to the backup call. The newly arrived officers were informed that the woman had been swimming, fully clothed, in the motel's pool, and that she appeared to be intoxicated on alcohol, drugs, or both. After leaving the pool, she had forced herself, using verbal threats and physical contact, into another person's room.

The three officers on the scene entered the room and found her on the phone. They ordered her to hang up. When she refused to do so, one officer crossed the room, took the phone from her hand, and hung it up. He then informed the woman that the manager of the hotel had said she was trespassing and that she would be placed under arrest if she did not leave the premises.

The woman then became very abusive, both verbally and physically. She slapped at the hands of one of the officers as he tried to escort her from the room, and shouted incoherently. She also punched one of the officers in the chest and began to kick the others.

As soon as the woman became violent, all three officers rushed her, subdued her, laid her on the bed, and forcibly handcuffed her.

They then placed her in the back seat of one of the patrol vehicles. She then began to kick the windows. As was the case during the incident described previously, the officers removed the woman from the car, tied her ankles and wrists together behind her back, and again placed her in the vehicle for transportation to jail.

As the officers were tying the woman, a man, later identified as her husband, pulled into the motel parking lot. He jumped from his vehicle and began to run toward the officers at full speed. One of the officers was turning to face him, abandoning the struggle with the woman, when an onlooker in the crowd stopped the man by grabbing him and prevented him from joining the fight. The third officer then turned back to the struggle with the woman, who was quickly subdued. She was again placed in a patrol vehicle and transported to jail.

Case #3

A social-service worker received a referral from a neighbor about a vulnerable elderly woman. She had visited the woman for the first time the prior week and was going back for a second visit accompanied by one of the authors. The worker found the woman sitting in front of her very dilapidated trailer/shack. There was a wire fence around the dirt area in the front. The woman sat inside the fence on what used to be an upholstered chair (only the springs remained). Her numerous cats and two dogs wandered around her and jumped on her lap. Cat food spilled out of boxes at her feet. A foul smell emanated from the house. She was disheveled and dirty and did not remember the worker from when she had visited the previous week.

The worker asked her how she was doing. She said, "Fine," but that she wanted to sell the house. When asked if she owned her home, she replied, "Not this house, my other one." When the worker asked where the other house was located, she said she did not know. When asked if she had any family in the area, she said that she did not. The worker then asked if she had friends she could call. The woman told her she did not think so. She told the worker that her phone and electricity had been cut off and that she was almost out of food. The social-service worker glanced up and into the doorway of the house, but did not go inside to check on the phone or the food supply. When asked if she had electricity, the woman contradicted herself by saying, "I think so. I don't remember." The woman proceeded to talk about her animals. After listening for a few minutes, the social-service worker told the woman she was going to leave and said good-bye.

Case #4

A social-service worker received a referral about a physically handicapped man who had recently moved to the area. She had made an initial visit a few days earlier and learned that the man was able to walk short distances with difficulty and had limited use of his arms. The man had told the social-service worker that his wife had divorced him two years earlier when he had become severely disabled. He had been living with his sister in another state, but she had "kicked him out of the house." The sister had driven him to his present location, rented an apartment for him, and left. The apartment was not equipped for handicapped tenants. He knew no one in the area. After the social-service worker first had visited with the man, she had made arrangements for him to receive in-home meals and assistance with personal care. She also had requested that applications for placement in assisted living be sent to his home. A worker from her office had gone to the home to deliver a food box in the interim. She was now returning to check on him.

When she arrived at the apartment, the worker found the man in bed. He seemed embarrassed and explained that he had been having difficulty sleeping at night, so he had just been staying in bed because he was too tired to get up. He apologized for his appearance and said that he could not get his shirt off and wanted to change it. She helped him take his shirt off and got him a clean one. She then asked if he had enough food to eat until the meals service started in approximately a week. He said yes, but that he was unable to reach some of the food, and that he was unable to open the refrigerator. "When I try I am too tired to eat afterward," he said. The worker checked the food and moved it so that it was more accessible. After checking in the refrigerator, she found some milk and asked if he would like some cereal. After he said yes, she brought it to him. She then explained that the services she had requested for him would take about a week to start and that he would have to be patient. She then asked if he had received the forms in the mail to request placement in an assisted-living facility. He said that he had not. She asked if he had picked up his mail.

He said that he had not because he did not know for certain where the mailbox was, but he thought it was on the other side of the apartment complex. If it was, he could not walk that far.

The worker then went and got the man's mail. She looked through it and found that the forms were there. She assisted him in filling them out and offered to mail them for him. She talked with him about some of the things that he could do to help make his situation better and encouraged him to do so. The worker then left, giving the man her phone number to call if "problems come up."

UNDERSTANDING AND EVALUATING THE WORK OF FRONTLINE PUBLIC SERVANTS: COMPETING VISIONS

The cases cited are not typical in the sense that all or even most police officers and social-service workers engage in such actions every day. However, they are representative in the sense that they embody the dilemmas of contemporary frontline public service. Simply asked, how can we evaluate what these frontline public servants did? How did they evaluate these situations and make their decisions? Depending on the standards used to evaluate and interpret what the police officers and social-service workers did in these cases, their actions can be variously understood as appropriate or illegitimate, *regardless of the similarity of the cases.*

In case #1, for example, the officers' actions can be assessed from a number of perspectives. Officers are allowed and expected to protect themselves from danger and their vehicles from damage; therefore, the decision to handcuff and ultimately tie up the woman can be seen as appropriate in relation to those goals. Further, society has decided that driving while intoxicated is a problem worth the investment of significant resources to counteract; the growth in special programs designed to combat drunk driving is a sign of the seriousness with which society views this issue. Accordingly, the decision to arrest the woman for impaired driving can be seen as appropriate. Similarly, department rules reward officers (particularly officers in special enforcement units) who have high arrest and conviction rates. The arrest, then, might be justified as an officer following department rules and norms. And, of course, the law itself defines drunken driving as a serious problem and empowers officers to arrest and jail those who do it. Thus, the police officers' actions can be seen as appropriate on many dimensions.

Interestingly, the two officers originally dispatched to the call did not justify the decision to arrest the woman on any of these grounds. In fact, they did not think the arrest decision was right *in and of itself.* While they were comfortable with the actions they took after the arrest decision was made (i.e., handcuffing her, dragging her into and out of the car, tying her wrists and ankles, etc.), they did not think that any of those actions should have been necessary *because they did not think the woman ought to have been arrested at all.* "This didn't have to happen," one of the officers noted. "She didn't have to go to jail."

The officers' reasoning was telling. In their view, the woman ought to have been allowed to go home, despite the fact that she had been driving while intoxicated, because she had been involved in a widely reported tragedy. This event, the officers argued, meant that she "deserved a break." They admitted that drunk driving was a problem, but noted that there were probably other drunk drivers on the road at the same time she was, and so their time and energies could be better spent hunting down people who "needed" to go to jail—i.e., people for whom time in jail might influence their drinking and driving habits. Justice, in their opinion, was not served by arresting the woman.

The officers were also angry with the drunk driving task force officer who "jumped" their call, made decisions with which they disagreed (although they admitted the department's rules gave him the right to make these decisions), and forced them to spend a significant amount of time handling a case they did not think was "right." This officer, they said, was known for jumping calls and trying to bump up his statistics. In short, they were critical both of the decision to arrest and of the way in which the decision was made.

In contrast, there was little controversy among the officers (or, for that matter, the bystanders) in the second case. Each of the officers was comfortable both with the decision to arrest the woman and with the means they used to accomplish this goal. Further, the crowd of onlookers (which was quite large; the incident occurred in the middle of the afternoon) was equally supportive of the officers' actions. Comments like "she's crazy" and "she just wouldn't listen" characterized their view of the incident.

When he was informed of his wife's actions, even the woman's husband was apologetic and deferential. The officers, the crowd, and even interested "others" were united, then, in their assessment that this was an appropriate and legitimate use of police power.

The social-service cases differ from the police cases in that the workers handled the situations alone. Accordingly, the only short-term evaluation of their actions and choices was their own self-assessment. Like the police examples, these two workers responded quite differently to similar situations. Not only are their responses different, the basis of the self-assessment of the workers differed markedly. Like the police examples, in both cases arguments can be made for and against the legitimacy and appropriateness of their actions and self-evaluations.

Case #3 raises significant questions about how public servants decide what goals they will attempt to achieve. The worker, for example, explained that her role was to serve as an investigator, not as a case manager. So, by implication, she had no specific responsibility to personally assist the client with her health and food. In her role as investigator, she further explained, she had determined that the elderly woman was vulnerable, and therefore she had submitted a petition to the public fiduciary to serve as a trustee for the woman. Ideally, she said, funds would be secured and managed so as to allow a residential placement. The worker then said that she thought that the public fiduciary might not take the case, however, because there was likely very little money involved. In any case, she said, it would take a long time.

In handling the case this way, the worker reported that she was following departmental policy. Her agency was not funded to offer direct services, only to investigate suspected cases of adult abuse, neglect, and exploitation. By petitioning the public fiduciary, she was attempting to get the woman, whom she felt was very vulnerable, some help. That same day, the worker went to the public fiduciary's office and asked about the status of the case. She was told that her case was one of hundreds and that it would take time. After this visit, the worker expressed frustration that seemingly nothing could be done.

Yet the worker did not personally check to see if the woman had any food or attempt to access any short-term services for her. Emergency food deliveries, for example, were available and accessible. It can be argued that it would be a reasonable community expectation that such actions would be taken. If this is the case, then her actions might be criticized according to standards that she never considered. On the other hand, if she had gotten more involved in direct assistance and case management, she might also be criticized for overreaching the role determined for her agency by the state legislature.

In case #4, the worker, according to departmental policy, was also an investigator, not a social worker. While she was not directly violating department policy, she certainly went beyond the strict definitions of her job in providing the sort of assistance that she did. Clearly, the handicapped man was helped by her visit and the assistance she provided. She not only provided direct help, she offered information and support to enable him to help himself. By doing more than her job required, she was able both to access the system of social services that the man needed and to remove practical barriers to his well-being. The worker felt good about the case and the way she handled it. She said when asked about it that she "just likes to see things through." She explained that if her other cases had not been in pretty good shape, she would not have been able to spend as much time as she had on this one. She took into account whether her choices that morning had the effect of denying anyone else her services.

Still, as with the prior case, the mandate to her agency was to investigate, not to provide social services. The legislature in her state did not fund her agency or her position to perform these tasks. As such, her actions might be criticized as being inconsistent with legislative intent and departmentally defined roles.

The strikingly different views about the appropriateness of these actions points to the central problem facing frontline public servants today: Whether or not we think what they are doing is legitimate and appropriate depends on the standards we use and what goals we want them to achieve. Political and social leaders, academics, clients, and public servants themselves often set goals that they think frontline public servants ought to achieve and then criticize them if they fail to achieve these goals—sometimes without considering the multiple cross-pressures that may limit the possibility of achieving them. Importantly, however, while others can criticize, frontline public servants have to act, often in environments that are politically, socially, and practically problematic.

What these workers need—and indeed what supervisors, political and social leaders, academics, and clients need as well—is a model of frontline public service that can account for the various cross-pressures workers face *and* that can provide evaluative standards through which the legitimacy and appropriateness of workers' actions can be evaluated. This model, if it is to be useful and useable, must reflect the realities of contemporary frontline public service as seen by the workers themselves. It is to this task that the rest of this book turns.

PLAN OF THE BOOK

This book develops and illustrates a model of street-level leadership that views public service from the perspective of the worker. Each chapter begins with a description of a situation confronted by one of the street-level workers we observed. This story is then used to illustrate the themes and ideas developed in the chapter. Chapter One introduces the core ideas, assumptions, and methodology which underlie our arguments and examines the context of contemporary street-level public service. Chapter Two considers the changing nature of worker discretion and the importance of assessing the legitimacy of workers' discretionary choices. It then assesses how well existing models of public service account for the realities of worker discretion and how they address the need for accountability. Chapter Three then builds and presents the model of street-level leadership. Chapter Four illustrates the model with examples and cases observed during the course of the research for this book. Chapter Five explores the implications of the model for workers, for their agencies, and for the governance system. Finally, it explores how street-level leadership can be fostered and developed by workers, organizations, citizens, and policy makers.

Acknowledgments

As with any project, this book could not have been completed without the assistance of many people. We would like to take this space to thank them for their help.

First, of course, are the many men and women we observed over the course of this research. Without their participation, assistance, and, at times, tolerance, this project could not have been undertaken, much less completed. Sergeant Paul Balance of the Huntsville, Alabama, Police Department deserves special mention in this role; however, all of the workers whom we observed and of whom we asked questions were crucial to the ideas generated in this book. We want to thank them for trusting us and allowing us to share their workdays and hear their thoughts and insights. They taught us, inspired us, and ultimately changed us in ways we could not have imagined. Additionally, we very much appreciate the many shift supervisors and department administrators who gave their permission for this research and accommodated our schedules.

A book like this also could not have been possible without the work of the many scholars on whose ideas it builds. Key among these are Michael Lipsky, Paul Hersey, Kenneth Blanchard, James MacGregor Burns, Henry Kass, Charles Goodsell, Larry Terry, Douglas Morgan, John Kirlin, and Terry Cooper. We also wish to thank Sage Publications for giving us permission to use portions of our article "Street-level leadership: Rethinking the role of public servants in contemporary governance" (1996, *American Review of Public Administration* 26(4), 457–475) in various sections of the text. Likewise, we want to acknowledge the *Criminal Justice Review* for giving us permission to use portions of our article, "Street-level leadership: Understanding community policing" (1994, *Criminal Justice Review* 19(2), 189–211).

This book and the research that shaped it also benefited from the help of a number of faculty colleagues, reviewers, students, and others. We are particularly appreciative of Joseph Cayer and Barbara McCabe of Arizona State University, Manfred Steger, Jamal Nassar, Tom Eimermann, and Carlos Parodi of Illinois State University, Erwin Hargrove of Vanderbilt University, Allan Spitz of the University of Alabama–Huntsville, Shane Mahoney of Eastern Washington University, Charles Goodsell of Virginia Polytechnic Institute and State University, and Terry Cooper of the University of Southern California. The financial and personal support of Anne Schneider and Dickinson McGaw of Arizona State University were of tremendous help at critical points in the research and in the development of the manuscript. The research and editorial assistance of Sandi Parkes and Heather Kettering, and the production assistance of Janet Soper and Mary Fran Draisker at Arizona State University were invaluable. Also, the Northwest Institute at Eastern Washington University provided financial support in the early days of this project, and we wish to thank them at this time for "taking a chance." Together, the ideas, insights, and support of all these individuals and organizations helped to shape this book's strengths. Its weaknesses, of course, are all our own.

Finally, we both wish to thank our families. Lane wants to thank Jim and Anne Crothers for a lifetime of love and support. Janet wishes to give special thanks to Douglas Vinzant for his love, encouragement, and many expressions of confidence in her and this book. She is also indebted to Ben and Mary Vinzant for their patience, hugs, and good humor—such wonderful children are a rare gift and are as greatly appreciated as they are loved.

1

The Context of Street-Level Public Service

"Every case is different." —a police officer during an observation

The Work of Street-Level Public Servants: The Case of the Drunken Street Brawl

While patrolling shortly after local bars closed one night, a police officer saw a man carrying a four-foot-long piece of pipe and running toward two groups of men arguing in the street. When they saw the police car, both groups and the man carrying the pipe ran around the corner.

The officer sped after them. After turning the corner, he saw that the groups were still arguing with each other. He also saw the man with the pipe nearing both groups. The officer stopped his car, jumped out, and pulled his gun. He ordered the man with the pipe to drop it, and ran to place himself between the two groups.

As soon as the officer pulled his gun, the man with the pipe dropped it, raised his hands, and yelled, "I'm not doing anything!" The two groups, however, were less compliant; individuals in both groups continued to shout taunts and threats at each other, even as the officer tried to separate them. Only when he was able to force members of both groups to stand on opposite sides of the street did the participants begin to relax and become responsive to his orders.

Once the groups were separated, the officer began investigating the incident. He talked with both groups, attempting to determine the source of the conflict and whether any crime

had been committed. When individual members of each group continued to make threats to the other group, he confronted them directly, ordering them to be quiet or face the consequences. Then, after he identified comparatively reasonable members of each group—those who were mostly attentive and responsive to his orders—he pulled them aside to discuss what had caused the fight and how it could be resolved. When, however, during one such conference a man from one of the groups began approaching the other while holding and shaking something in his hand, the officer immediately changed his behavior—he pulled his gun, pointed it at the man, and ordered him back to his side of the street. (It later turned out that the man was jiggling his keys.)

Later, once the fight had been cleared up and the combatants had been sent home (going, on his order, in separate directions), the officer explained that as simple as it was to break up the fight, deciding what to do about it was complex. At first, each group of men wanted to press charges on the other for assault. No one in either group, however, was injured, and, with the exception of the man with the pipe, none had committed a crime in the officer's presence. Further, all the participants were intoxicated. Thus, arresting any or all of them would have involved investing a great deal of his and other officers' time, as well as society's resources, on what amounted to intoxicated people behaving stupidly.

At the same time, however, the law was clear: assault is a crime. Further, the fight had to be resolved, preferably without calling several other officers out of their patrol zones, thereby leaving their areas unprotected.

To achieve what he thought was the best outcome to the situation, the officer worked with both groups until most of them admitted it was a "stupid fight" and promised not to continue it once he left. The officer also had the "reasonable" people in both groups shake hands. Then the groups went their separate ways and the officer resumed his patrol.

INTRODUCTION

This book is about street-level public servants and how they can successfully and effectively meet the challenges of their very difficult jobs. It is also about how we, as citizens, academicians, public managers, and policy makers, define what they do and view their role in the governance system. In communities across America, public employees grapple with some of the most critical and pressing problems facing society. They are on the front lines and in the streets, working to protect the vulnerable, reunite troubled families, apprehend criminals, fight drug abuse, curb gangs, and keep kids in school. Obviously, the manner in which these workers understand and carry out their responsibilities is vitally important to individual citizens, communities, and the nation.

Yet, despite numerous theories, relatively little is known about how these workers view their jobs, what they actually do, and how they can do it better. This book is an effort to begin to fill this knowledge gap. It proceeds from the premise that the theory and language we use to understand and talk about street-level public service exerts a powerful influence over how workers view themselves and their responsibilities; how agencies recruit, train, and manage these employees; and ultimately, how society defines the role these workers play in the governance process. This book does not and cannot provide any easy answers or pat formulas for meeting the challenges of street-level public service. The work that these individuals do is simply too complex and too important for such approaches. Instead, it is a systematic attempt to bridge the gap between existing theory and the realities of the street, and in the process, to further develop and refine the theoretical lenses we use to view street-level public service.

Why is the work of street-level public servants so complicated and difficult? There are a number of reasons. First, police officers, social-service workers, and other frontline public employees confront a wide variety of complex and unpredictable problems and situations. In the course of their work, for example, a child protective services worker may be called upon to take custody of a child, calm a distraught teenager, do an initial physical examination of an injured child, work with police in investigating sexual abuse, console a hysterical child, counsel a concerned grandparent, interview a reluctant first grader, assess the dangers in a filthy home, confront a drug-addicted mom, testify in court, and educate an angry father. A police officer, in the course of a single shift, may defuse a street fight, track down a robbery suspect, counsel teenagers on the corner, issue a speeding ticket, manage a domestic-violence situation, arrest a suspect wielding a weapon, respond to a burglar alarm, and try to calm people in crisis. These workers often do not know when and how such situations will occur. As one worker put it, "There are common themes, there are common problems, but every situation is different. You just never know what you're going to be dealing with until you're in the middle of it."

Second, not only is there great variation and unpredictability in the problems these workers face, but the problems themselves are often multifaceted, intractable, and emotionally laden. On a daily basis, these workers confront problems that, put simply, no one has figured out how to solve. Worse, these problems do not present themselves singly. It is not unusual for a single case or situation to involve, at least to some degree, criminal activity, social-service issues, mental health concerns, substance abuse issues, and medical matters. Workers must assess these situations and decide which problems to deal with, how they will respond, and who should be involved.

Third, street-level public servants confront a decision-making context that is complicated, fluid, and politically charged. They may be working with clients who are compliant, combative, or passive. They may have limited information, resources, and time. Precise agency rules may or may not govern what the worker ought to do. Federal, state, and local laws may be consistent or seem to conflict on a given matter. Family members, a few bystanders, or large crowds may gather to watch and attempt to influence a situation's outcome. And, of course, individual workers may have personal values that run counter to what the client wants or needs, the agency requires, the community demands, and/or the law dictates.

In the middle of all these pressures, street-level public servants are expected to make decisions that will achieve the agency's, the community's, and the broader society's goals. Deciding what to do under such complicated circumstances is problematic at best. Yet the problems they confront must be dealt with, even while the worker knows that his or her efforts will usually fall far short of "fixing" them.

As will be discussed more fully in the pages that follow, existing conceptions of public service view workers as bureaucrats, policy makers, power wielders, problem solvers, professionals, and/or political actors. Each of these models offers important insights, but none adequately captures the realities and complexities of contemporary frontline public service. They do not provide an adequate basis for understanding the challenges frontline workers face, are not fully descriptive of what workers do in response to those challenges, and do not suggest a framework for evaluating the appropriateness of worker choices.

In this book, we argue that the concept of leadership provides a more appropriate and useful framework for understanding what frontline workers do and ought to do. It is an argument that is grounded in over 1,500 hours of direct observations of these workers in four states over several years. We examine the types of challenges these workers actually confront, the factors they must consider, and the hard choices they have to make. Based on this examination, we argue that the street-level leadership model provides a positive, realistic, and constructive portrayal of frontline public service.

The basis of these arguments is detailed in the chapters which follow, but can be outlined here in very summary form. Leadership is typically associated with individuals who occupy the top positions in organizations, communities, and societies. Indeed, unless one is thinking of street gangs, grassroots social and political movements, and the like, the pairing of "street" and "leadership" may seem incongruous. This pairing may seem all the more improbable given that the topic of this book is leadership as practiced by line-level public servants—i.e., those public employees who serve at the relative *bottoms* of their organizations and physically deliver services to the public. Such workers defy common conceptions of leadership. So how, then, are frontline public servants "leaders"?

While the fit is not perfect, based upon a careful analysis of the work performed by street-level public servants and an examination of existing conceptions of their role, we argue that what street-level workers do can often be best understood as leadership. Leadership is found to be an appropriate and useful theoretical framework for several reasons. First, like their executive-level counterparts, street-level workers exercise discretion and judgment in complex, fluid environments. Second, the choices made by leaders and workers are often difficult and have important consequences for individuals, organizations, and communities. Third, like leaders, frontline workers decide what to do and how to do it based on a range of circumstantial and other factors in the context of values, norms, and other constraints. So, their actions not only influence, but are also influenced by, numerous factors. Fourth, in the same way that leaders often exercise power, frontline public servants also have a great deal of power. In both cases, however, the exercise of that power must be legitimate if the leader's choices and behavior are considered to be an act of leadership. In other words, while leaders do exercise power, it is power that must be constrained, accountable, and limited by a complex mix of norms, values, laws, and other factors. If it is not, then it is simply power, manipulation, coercion, or something else—not leadership.

Thus, because the notion of leadership embodies questions of discretion, power, and legitimacy, it can be used as the theoretical foundation for understanding what frontline workers do and for evaluating the appropriateness and effectiveness of their choices. The concept of leadership captures both the importance of their work and the significance of their role in the governance system. For these and other reasons that will be discussed more fully in the chapters which follow, we suggest that street-level public servants are, or at least can be, leaders—with all the potential, opportunity, and responsibility that the concept entails.

CORE IDEAS AND ASSUMPTIONS

Before expanding on the components of this argument, it is important to make clear a number of core ideas and assumptions.[1] The first of these is that *the work of line-level public employees is important.* As is discussed in detail later in this chapter, such workers face some of the most intractable and pervasive problems in contemporary American society. The manner in which these workers view their responsibilities and carry out programs and policies is important both to the individuals involved and, potentially, to society at large. Worker choices can profoundly influence the lives of their clients, their families, members of a neighborhood or community, and, by extension, the entire nation. What these workers do, then, deserves serious attention and consideration.

Second, because of the nature of their work, many street-level public servants regularly exercise significant amounts of discretion as they do their jobs. As will be seen, discretion is absolutely essential if these

---

1. It should be made clear here that not all street-level public servants face complex decision-making situations. Moreover, as will be discussed later in this chapter, not all such workers exercise significant amounts of discretion as they do their jobs. This research focuses primarily on that set of workers who both encounter difficult decisions and regularly use discretion as they do their jobs.

workers are to do their jobs successfully and effectively. Discretion, however, can be used appropriately and beneficially, can be used inappropriately and for the wrong reasons, and can be outright abused. It is important to study how and why workers exercise their discretion if we are to understand and evaluate line-level public servants in action.

Third, the importance of discretion in public service, combined with its potential for both benefit and abuse, raises questions about the legitimacy of worker action. Given what are often crosscutting pressures of individual preferences, client desires, institutional rules, legal standards, and cultural norms, there is almost always at least some principle upon which the appropriateness of specific worker actions can be challenged. In order to be fair to workers and to give them the tools they need to do their jobs, it is essential to develop a means by which the legitimacy of their choices can be established and demonstrated.

Fourth, because of the dynamic nature of both discretion and legitimacy, there may be multiple choices available to workers in any given situation. Moreover, many of these alternatives might be seen as appropriate by some standard. The work these individuals do, then, is not always a matter of achieving some single, preferred goal. Instead, workers may choose among several possible, legitimate options. Understanding why they make the choices they do is essential if we are to promote effective decision making by street-level public servants.

The book also embodies some implicit assumptions that should be made as clear as possible. First, the book has two purposes, one descriptive and the other prescriptive. At one level, it is an attempt to describe the working environment of particular types of street-level public servants in a way that adequately captures the factors that can be shown to influence their behavior. The decision-making environment in which workers operate, it will be seen, is substantially more complex than is generally recognized. Consequently, any attempt to understand why and how workers make the choices they do must be informed by a more sophisticated awareness of the factors that influence them if it is to be useful.

Prescriptively, the book builds a model of street-level leadership from the description of what workers do. The street-level leadership model is shown to describe how workers make choices, to provide prescriptive tools to aid workers in doing a more effective job, and to provide standards for evaluating worker actions. In short, the book has a dual purpose, both to describe what is and to suggest what ought to be.

Further, this book is written from the perspective of the worker and therefore adopts a "worker-centered" approach. This has several important implications. Many, if not most, studies of public employees are written from the standpoint of the manager and the organization. As a result, problems and solutions are identified largely at the organizational level. This book describes public service from the viewpoint of workers; it defines the environment, the challenges, and the demands of *their* work from *their* perspective. So, while there are important implications of these worker perspectives for public organizations, the policy-making process, and the larger governance system, this book is not intended as a management review of public organizations or a critique of the policy process. Instead, it takes the context of street-level public services largely as a "given" and attempts to illuminate how workers view this environment and how they work effectively within it.

The worker-centered perspective of this book also has methodological implications. As is discussed later in this chapter, the methodology used for this study was participant observation. This was judged to be the best way to develop an understanding of what workers were actually doing and how they were doing it. As a consequence, the book reflects, to the greatest degree possible, a view of street-level public service as defined by the workers themselves. Although this approach was judged to be the most appropriate, given the purposes of the book, it does have some weaknesses that ought to be noted.

For example, one of the consequences of this methodological approach was that the researchers came to know, admire, and identify with the workers.[2] As a result, the book reflects a bias in favor of street-level public servants. Although every attempt was made to maintain a level of objectivity, in almost all cases the authors came to appreciate and respect the workers whom they observed. The work these people do is hard, complicated, and relatively thankless. The vast majority of public service workers observed in this study were found to be serious, dedicated people

---

2. This can also be seen as a strength in qualitative research, as the establishment of relationships with subjects is important in the data-collection process.

trying to do their best. While there were cases of what can be seen as failure, these were the exception rather than the rule. Thus, rather than emerging with a cynical attitude about what such workers do, this book manifests a generally optimistic tone. There are certainly problems in street-level public service; however, taken as a whole, the individuals who do this difficult work appear to be trying their best to "do the right thing" and make the world a better place.

Finally, while it is the case that workers are seen here as the center of activity, it is important to emphasize that we do not in any way suggest that they are exempted from any kinds of social, legal, organizational, or ethical constraints. That is, in contrast to some analyses of worker discretion that seem to validate worker choices as such (most notably Michael Lipsky's 1980 book *Street-Level Bureaucracy)*, this book does not argue that just because workers have to exercise discretion, whatever they do with that discretion is legitimate. Instead, this book places workers in a matrix of influences that contextualizes their actions *but also establishes criteria toward which they can reasonably be expected to act and by which they may be evaluated appropriately.* In short, discretionary choices, however necessary they may be, are not inevitably right.

This chapter begins to develop these ideas by first discussing the role and significance of street-level public servants in the governance system of the United States. Second, it addresses the forces that can be shown to influence the decisions they make. Finally, it explains the methodology and approach of the study that served as the basis of the book. From this foundation, the model of street-level leadership will be explained and demonstrated in the work of several different types of street-level public servants.

WHAT STREET-LEVEL PUBLIC SERVANTS DO AND WHY IT MATTERS

In order to more fully understand how and why frontline public servants are, or can be, leaders, it is necessary to accurately describe what they do—i.e., what their role is in the broader system of governance in the United States. After all, no model can be either descriptive or usefully prescriptive if it is not solidly grounded in the circumstances it claims to describe. Thus, the work of street-level public servants in contemporary America must be closely examined before a new model of their actions can be developed.

At one level, understanding the role of street-level public servants in the broader system of governance in the United States is quite simple: such workers execute the rules, programs, and policies established by their agencies in accordance with the law. Although it may be obvious, it is worth stating that once laws are passed, someone has to implement them. Public programs, or at least most of them, are not self-executing. Public employees, then, are needed to process claims, answer calls, and deliver whatever services the law has authorized.

In the cases observed during the research for this book, for example, street-level public servants investigated allegations of physical and sexual child abuse, answered accident calls, responded to burglaries, intervened in cases of domestic violence, counseled the mentally disturbed, removed children from neglectful parents, testified in court, arrested felons, educated families, defused riots, coordinated services, placed vulnerable adults in residential placements, stopped suspected drunk drivers, engaged in high-speed pursuits, and established control over murder scenes. In each case, workers were simply implementing societal dictates; laws granted workers the authority to take these actions, and the bureaucracies they worked for had developed procedures and expectations that led them to undertake such activities.

This simple accounting for what workers do does not fully capture their significance in the governance system, however. At the very least, it implies that workers are funnels through whom public policies are poured unaffected. This, at best, is a parody of what workers actually do. It certainly does not seem to account for the complexities dealt with by the police officer whose story starts this chapter. As will be demonstrated throughout this book, there are often multiple and conflicting expectations and pressures that shape what workers do. What street-level public servants *do*, in effect, is make choices both about the factors of influence that ought to be given the most attention in a given situation and about the actions that these influences require. That is, workers operate in a context established by law, organizational rules, and so forth, but they interpret what these influences mean in specific cases. Street-level public servants, in other words, deliver public goods and services *as they find appropriate, given the circumstances at hand*. Rather than being ciphers, then, workers are active participants in the governance system.

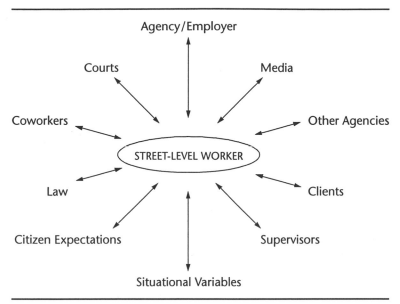

Figure 1. Influences on Street-Level Public Servants

Mapping the Environment of Contemporary Street-Level Public Service

In order to more fully understand the argument that workers are meaningful actors in the governance process, it is necessary to explore the influences that shape their work. Figure 1 depicts the diverse variables that can be seen to influence the choices that street-level public servants make. Based on the observations made for this book, it provides a *partial* list of the kinds of factors that can be shown to shape worker decisions.

As depicted, workers are in the center of a matrix of influences. Some of these influences are straightforward, while others can exercise an indirect influence on workers. Additionally, these variables can be at cross-purposes both within themselves and with each other. Each, however, can be seen to regularly influence how and why street-level public servants do what they do. (Note that the description of the variables that follows is, after "street-level worker," offered in alphabetical order. Rather than presenting a hierarchy of influences, then, this section simply expands on Figure 1 and leaves open the possibility that different factors will have more or less weight in different circumstances.)

Street-Level Worker

This is the individual employee or employees who make decisions in a specific case at a particular time. In this book, street-level public employees (also referred to as "frontline" or "line-level" public servants or workers to avoid excessive repetitiveness in the text) are those who are directly responsible for service delivery to the public and who exercise a significant level of discretion in carrying out their responsibilities. These are the same categories of workers dealt with in Lipsky's seminal work on street-level bureaucracy (1980), particularly police officers and social-service workers. Individual workers bring to the job a particular mix of factors and characteristics that may influence how they perceive situations and react to them (Kroeger 1975; Stone 1981; Pugh 1986; Delattre 1989). These factors may include personality traits, moral values, experiences, ethnicity, gender, religious beliefs, educational background, work experience, professional affiliation, culture, role definitions, and the like. For example, holding other factors constant, a person who has personally experienced spousal or family abuse in the past may respond differently when confronted with a domestic-violence situation than a person who has not.

Agency/Employer

This category includes the agency or organization for which the public servant works. Organizational constraints and characteristics have been argued to exert a significant level of influence over the exercise of worker discretion (Peyrot 1982; Reuss-Ianni and Ianni 1983; Franz and Jones 1987; Harrison and Pelletier 1987; Scott 1997). Influences on workers' decision making include, for example, agency rules, goals, evaluation mechanisms, authority relationships, and training guidelines. Thus, rules regarding overtime may influence a police officer's decision to make an arrest at the end of a shift. Or a social-service worker may be influenced in determining the disposition of a case if he or she knows that the performance evaluation system is based, in part, on the number of cases closed. Organizational culture, as the embodiment of an organization's generally held norms and values, also exerts an important influence on worker discretion (Kelly 1994). Organizational culture shapes workers' choices by influencing their underlying predispositions and preferences about their roles and purposes in their jobs (Kaufman 1960; Schein 1992). For example, the culture in one organization may value independent actions by workers, while the culture in another organization may emphasize a more consultative approach. Workers who violate such organizational norms are subject to criticism, ostracism, or sanction.

Clients

Clients are those individuals with whom street-level public servants have a statutory or programmatic responsibility to work. In a given situation, there may be more than one client or set of clients. For example, the primary clients in a child-abuse case may be the child and the parents. Secondarily, however, the grandparents who temporarily care for the child and the school officials who made the referral can also be seen as clients potentially in need of information, guidance, support, or services. Clients may be suspects, prisoners, child molesters, children, homeless people, students, drug addicts, victims, patients, or parents—in this book, all are referred to as clients. These clients influence workers' decisions, both directly and indirectly (Goodsell 1980; Weimann 1982; Franklin 1985; Weakland and Jordan 1992; Scott 1997). Clients' demands for or refusal of service, their demeanor, their values and expectations can all be seen to affect what workers do and how they do it. A compliant client may elicit a different kind of response than a belligerent one would. Client characteristics such as race, gender, and class can also influence workers directly or as they interact with other factors like the worker's own race, gender, class, experience, and training.

Coworkers

Coworkers are the worker's peers or associates within the agency. They may be assigned to work together or may simply consult with each other on occasion. Coworkers can also be those with whom the worker regularly interacts during the course of their jobs such as dispatchers, intake workers, or secretaries. Relationships with coworkers have been shown to be important to worker satisfaction (Ting 1996; DeSantis and Durst 1996). Beyond issues of worker satisfaction, however, coworkers exert influence on each other in several ways. First, coworkers may offer suggestions, support, or criticism to a worker. A coworker may be important in helping a worker "let off steam" and thereby managing the stress that may influence how a worker responds to a given set of circumstances. In law enforcement and child protective services, coworkers may also tend to spend time together in social situations. These coworkers may feel ostracized by others and know that they can better understand the stresses and frustrations they face, as well as the need to relax and laugh. Not surprisingly, these relationships influence how workers approach their jobs. Second, coworkers often provide an important and immediate sort of feedback and evaluation of a worker's choices (Greller 1980). This evaluation may be known or unknown to the worker, but most workers consider the expected reaction of coworkers in making decisions. The influence of coworkers is also crucial in terms of the information they provide to street-level workers. For example, a dispatcher or intake worker may or may not correctly classify a call, or a coworker may or may not offer information on his/her previous experiences with a particular client. Such information may directly influence how a worker makes choices about a particular situation or case.

Community

Community, as used here, means the local environment in which the street-level public servant is acting. This can include neighborhoods, towns, cities, or counties—each of which may exercise a different kind of influence on the worker's choices. For example, one neighborhood may want the police to actively patrol for and pursue burglary suspects, while in another area citizens may want only police assistance and support in establishing a "neighborhood watch" program to combat the same problem. These preferences can directly affect worker choices because they establish what the community demands from the agency and the worker (Trojanowicz and Moore 1988; Magill 1979). Such preferences also may have an indirect influence as they are integrated into agency operations and training programs. The dominant cultural influences of a community can also be important. Because culture encompasses a set of relatively shared ideas, ideals, concepts, stories, and myths that orient people within their social and political environment, culture helps to explain how and why people act as they do within a given community (Douglas 1970; Thompson, Ellis, and Wildavsky 1990; Douglas 1982). If the worker fails to act as the dominant culture expects, this failure may result in a number of repercussions. For example, it may cause members of the community to become belligerent or uncooperative. Important information or access may be withheld. As a result, workers need to consider these factors in making choices about how to handle a particular situation.

Courts

Federal, state, and local courts can be seen to have significant influences on what workers do (Rosenbloom and Carroll 1990; Schroeder 1995; Reamer 1994; Hegar 1988; Lee and Hull 1983; Alexander and Alexander 1995; Howing and Wodarski 1992; Kutchens 1991; Bernstein and McCutchan 1983). Courts, for example, exercise considerable indirect influence over workers as they interpret rules and laws, establish the civil rights and liberties of clients, shape the types of tools that agencies and workers can use to achieve their goals, and define criteria that constrain worker choices. Courts can also exercise a direct influence on workers as they consider what courts may or may not do in response to the situation the worker is facing. Workers who do not consider or observe the formal and informal rules of the judicial system can be informally sanctioned. A prosecutor may refuse to take a criminal case or a judge may not listen sympathetically to a petition from a social-service worker. Knowledge of this potential can then indirectly affect the worker's choices.

Law

Law grants the statutory authority under which workers operate. It establishes the budgets that support the agency's capacity to perform its functions; it frames the structure of an agency and its operations; and it defines an agency's, and thereby to some degree the worker's, goals. To a greater or lesser degree, it influences program design, implementation, and evaluation. Law can directly influence workers' choices by authorizing, requiring, or curtailing action. It can also indirectly influence workers through its impact on agency mission, evaluation systems, and community expectations.

Media

Television, radio, newspapers, and magazines can also shape what street-level public servants do. The simple presence of television cameras at a scene can encourage bystanders to change their behavior or can lead individual workers to behave more formally with each other than they otherwise might. In addition, heightened media coverage of either a specific incident or a type of case may encourage workers, agencies, courts, legislators, and communities to pay more attention to some cases (Lutrin and Settle 1992) and, consequently, shape what workers decide to do.

Other Service or Provider Agencies

Commonly, street-level public servants have to work with other agencies to do their jobs. They may not be called until some other agency notifies them of a case, or they may be dependent on other service providers to fully complete the work involved in a single case. This knowledge may shape workers' decisions about whether to take action if they do not think that they can garner support from such follow-up agencies, or it may affect how they present cases to other agencies in the first place. Additionally, the existence of and relationship between the worker's agency/employer and other agencies may shape departmental rules, operating procedures, and the like—all of which will influence worker choices.

Situational Variables

Situational variables include whatever other factors influence the worker in a particular circumstance. Such factors can have a significant influence on worker behavior (Worden 1989). This category may include things such as the weather, how busy the worker is, whether or not bystanders are present and how hostile or helpful they are, or whether it is dark. Such factors may immediately influence worker decisions; if, for example, a police officer sees a minor offense on a busy shift, such an offense might be ignored. On another shift it might be treated more seriously simply because of the priority an officer can give the call under specific circumstances.

Supervisors

Finally, a worker's immediate supervisor can affect his or her decisions (O'Looney 1996; Reuss-Ianni and Ianni 1983; Thibault, Lynch, and McBride 1990; Sparrow 1988; Kadushin 1985; Brashears 1995; Weinbach 1984). Supervisors can establish explicit expectations for performance, in terms of both category and volume. Supervisors also have expectations for how and when workers will consult them. They have differing preferences for how much information they want from workers and preferred worker styles and approaches. Additionally, supervisors often conduct personnel evaluations, recommend or provide additional training and advice, and strongly influence if not control work assignments, promotions, and salary adjustments. As a result, their preferences, expectations, and values are a major consideration in what workers do.

Complexity in Action

Cumulatively, these direct and indirect influences can be seen to regularly shape what workers do and how they do it. Of course, different variables may have greater or lesser influence in different circumstances. Further, the factors depicted in Figure 1 may vary in importance for different workers in the same incident. As a result, the interaction between these variables can be extraordinarily complex and somewhat unpredictable.

Take, for example, the case that leads this chapter. At least some, if not all, of the variables presented in Figure 1 were observed to straightforwardly influence the officer's decision making. The law, for example, was clearly a factor: assault is a crime. Accordingly, the incident could not be ignored and the officer had the legal right to detain and question the participants about their activities. Next, the agency's rules and society's laws empowered and even required the officer to intervene and attempt to stop the assaults or to arrest the perpetrators. Agency norms were also fairly clear: officers who backed off from confrontations were disparaged. In addition, citizens expect the police to protect public safety. Officers who drive by major disturbances of public order would be violating this expectation.

It is also the case that the officer made it quite clear that he perceived it was his responsibility to end the fight. In this way, his personal norms and preferences affected his actions. Further, the clients expressed clear expectations about what ought to be done, and their behaviors directly shaped what the officer did. In addition, the worker's situational assessment of the seriousness of the incident, the likelihood of its recurrence without his intervention, and his responsibilities under the law as a police officer directly influenced the amount of time he spent working on the incident and its resolution.

There were also a number of indirect influences on the officer's decision making. Based on his experience, for example, the officer explained that courts generally treated cases of "group assault" by bar patrons as a less serious offense than other kinds of crimes—particularly when the participants were all intoxicated and no one was injured. So while he might have had authority to arrest the brawlers, he assumed that the probability of their being charged or convicted was quite low. Moreover, while citizens expect police officers to protect public safety, the officer noted that generally they do not want their tax money spent on unproductive arrests. In addition, they do not want several different officers pulled out of their patrol zones in order to answer a pointless call. As a consequence, ensuring public safety, which could be done in this case by the arrest and removal of the specific individuals engaged in the fight, was not the only variable the officer had to consider in deciding what to do. In fact, at one extreme, it is possible to argue that the officer should have walked away from the fight entirely—time spent dealing with intoxicated citizens who had committed no obvious crimes was time not spent checking buildings for burglaries, stopping driving-under-the-influence (DUI) suspects, and so on.

There were additional indirect influences as well. The officer's supervisor had a "handle it" philosophy. He expected his officers to do their jobs with minimal involvement on his or their colleagues' parts. Also, the same organizational norms that criticized officers for backing down from fights also pressured officers to handle confrontations on their own, without the assistance of fellow officers. And the law regarding assault was sufficiently vague that there was no clear ground, given the other influences on his decision, to arrest the combatants. Accordingly, the officer chose to work with the participants until they had calmed down and he felt that he could send them on their separate ways with little fear that the fight would restart.

In the end, then, the officer's decision about how to handle the incident was the result of several different variables. As is suggested in Figure 1, the worker was at the center of a matrix of influences. His decision making was complicated by the fact that these influences directed him in different ways—some factors encouraged arrest, for example, while others discouraged it. Further, some variables were unclear in their influence—i.e., the public's desires for safety, efficiency, and effective patrolling. But regardless of the multiple and conflicting pressures on him, the officer had to make decisions on the spot. Ultimately, in making the choices he made, the officer, in effect, interpreted a mix of laws, rules, preferences, and values and decided how they ought to be applied in this particular case.

Influence, Governance, and Street-Level Public Servants

As will be made clear throughout the rest of this book, the types of actions that the officer took, the types of influences that shaped the officer's choices, and the significance of these actions and decisions for the broader system of governance in the United States is typical of the work of many street-level public servants. What workers often *do* is balance multiple and sometimes conflicting standards and expectations in making judgments about what to do in specific cases. Rather than simply carrying out society's dictates, workers interpret and apply these dictates dynamically and interactively to the circumstances they face. They may do this well or they may do it badly. Alternatively, some may think the worker has done a good job while others become critical and still others remain indifferent. In any case, workers can be seen as active participants in the process as they assess situations, choose how to respond, and, to some extent, determine outcomes.

Importantly, by making such judgments, in a very real sense these workers help to define what it means to be a citizen in America. Thus the questions of why and how workers make the choices they do is an important one in the governance system. Accordingly, understanding, evaluating, and ultimately shaping their decision making in ways the broader society desires is also important.

It is this vision of what workers do, and the environment in which they do it, that informs this work. The decision-making environment described in Figure 1 provides the "stuff" with which workers work, from which they have to make choices and construct solutions as they do their jobs. This is a difficult and problematic task, of course, but it is both a curse and an opportunity. This environment makes it possible for workers to have a significant positive influence over involved individuals and society at large. However, it also makes it possible to make bad judgments and create negative consequences for both clients and communities.

METHODOLOGY AND APPROACH

In order to build a model of frontline public service grounded in the realities of street-level public service, the authors employed a methodological approach that warrants some special discussion. Put simply, the arguments and claims made in this book are derived from direct observations of dozens of street-level public servants in various agencies and in diverse communities. Accordingly, the stories told and the conclusions drawn in the course of this work are asserted to accurately describe the real working environments that shape what street-level public servants do and to provide useful data that can be generalized across a variety of programs, agencies, and communities. In order to make the case for these assertions, however, it is necessary to explain the study's methodology in a little more detail.

The authors conducted over 1,500 hours of direct observation of street-level public servants in four states. Approximately 100 workers in total were observed.[3] The methodology used was participant observation. The authors used an approach that has been described as "grounded theory" (Glaser and Strauss 1967). As the observations were conducted, the authors identified similarities and differences across cases, and constantly checked their emerging ideas and models against the observations. The analysis of these observations was interpretive as described by Giddens (1976), in that theoretical structures for understanding social action were constructed based on observation and the articulation of meaning by the actors themselves.

As will be explained more fully in the sections which follow, the observations were neither comprehensive nor completely random. The intent was to study frontline public servants who exercised discretion in complex, difficult, and fluid environments. While the observers accompanied the workers throughout their normal workday, which included routine tasks such as filling out paperwork for most of them, the focus was on situations requiring the employees to make choices and exercise discretion. When time allowed before and after these situations or events, workers were

---

3. There were two levels of observation. The first level was workers with whom the observers rode for the duration of the workers' shifts. The second level was the workers who were also present at situations confronted during those rides. Thus, the number of workers is given as approximate to reflect the fact that some relatively brief (one-hour or so) observations were made of workers that are not reflected in the count of workers observed. On the other hand, some of these second-level observations were significant enough (observations of these workers over several days in a variety of situations while never actually riding with them) to be included in the total.

encouraged to describe the characteristics of the situation, the constraints and factors that they considered in responding, how they evaluated their response, and how they expected others to evaluate their approach. These responses were assessed to determine whether the worker perceived the situation as requiring discretion, what kind of discretion (if any) was exercised, and whether the reported decision-making process and evaluation of the event could be understood within the framework of street-level leadership.

As an approach, participant observation has a number of strengths that make it a particularly useful tool for the research undertaken here. In particular, participant observation is appropriate when there is a special interest in human meaning and interaction as viewed from the perspective of the actors themselves, when the work is focused on the here and now of everyday life situations and settings, when theorizing stresses interpretation and understanding, and when the context of action is important (Jorgensen 1989; Johnson 1975; Johnson and Joslyn 1986; Fenno 1978; Ross and Ross 1974).

The analysis undertaken here clearly fits these criteria. This is best demonstrated by a discussion of the process by which this study developed, for its history was a significant influence on its outcome. Ultimately, like Charles Goodyear's discovery of the vulcanization of rubber, this study emerged from a happy accident that led in often-unforeseen directions. As a consequence, it did not initially derive from a preexisting theory that was tested against real-world experiences. Instead, it was grounded theory, developed through a process that was first iterative and evolutionary; once established, it became more deductive and formal.

Genesis

Although it was not clear at the time, this book began in the winter/spring of 1991 when a student approached one of the authors at the end of a first-day-of-the-semester lecture and identified himself as a police officer. He continued by explaining that he worked third shift—10:00 p.m. to 6:00 a.m.—and so might occasionally miss the early morning class if he was held over or was particularly tired. This introduction served as the foundation for an invitation that followed a few weeks later—an invitation to accompany the officer on an observational ride-along as he worked one of his shifts. After a few days' consideration, the author agreed, and the first link in the chain of events that led to this book was forged.

That first ride was both interesting and fateful. In the course of a single Saturday night's shift, the officer responded to an automobile accident in which a woman had lost control of her car, run it into a ditch, and trapped herself against a telephone pole so seriously that it took rescuers forty-five minutes to get her out; answered a "shots fired" call at a condominium complex by walking into a crowd of people running through a parking lot—only to discover that the "shots" were firecrackers; and participated—after an extended, 100+ miles-per-hour drive to get to the scene—in the capture of a burglary suspect who had been videotaped inside a school stealing from one of its vending machines. In fact, all of these events had taken place by 3:00 a.m., just five hours into the officer's shift.

What emerged from this original ride-along was an informal pattern of observations in which the author called the officer, or vice versa, to suggest a ride on a given night. This informality turned out to be significant as a manifestation of the fact that this research began with no preset or established theoretical predisposition. Indeed, it did not even start out as a research project at all—it was simply an opportunity to experience interesting nights, seeing a dimension of society that many people never know.

Concept Development and Refinement

As these observational ride-alongs continued, it became clear that the cases being observed held a treasure trove of data that could be applied to a research project. At first, models of organizational culture were considered for theoretical direction in shaping the research—the particular police department in which research was conducted had an interesting organizational culture that could be seen to shape officer behavior in important ways. Thus, the original plan was to develop a case study of the agency under question to illustrate and develop models of organizational culture.

As observations continued, however, it became clear that models of organizational culture did not fully capture what officers did during their shifts. After all, one of the central assumptions of such models is that the character of an agency—its rules, norms, and mores—causes, or at least significantly shapes, worker activities.

While this assumption often bears out empirically, it cannot easily account for deviance—cases in which officers defy the culture or use their own judgments in deciding how to handle a specific case. Yet workers were observed to regularly take such actions. Additionally, the assumptions inherent in organizational culture models did not seem to readily account for other variables, like community values, moral standards, and client behaviors, that were seen to influence the decisions that officers made. Organizational culture, then, was clearly part of the story, but it was not the end.

Moreover, it became increasingly clear that other existing models of worker roles and responsibilities were also inadequate to explain what the observer was seeing. It was while driving with a police officer under a bridge late one night/early one morning that a "eureka" moment occurred: police officers, as they do their jobs, act as leaders. They often make choices about what ought to be done; they may select among alternative means for achieving these goals; they can be seen to negotiate with clients, supervisors, and even other agencies about what objectives should be sought and how they should be realized; and, ultimately, their choices shape the sanctions and rewards that society can levy against its citizens. Indeed, in this sense officer choices appeared to lead society. In making decisions about how to apply the community's rules in individual cases, officers led the community to action in specific circumstances.

The idea that police officers may be seen as acting like leaders caused a significant shift in the research for this book. It was at this point that the second researcher joined the project and a search began for a model of leadership that might account for what police officers do. Additionally, the observational ride-alongs took on a different focus—rather than examining the ways the organization's culture affected officers' choices, attention was focused on understanding the multiple forces that shaped officer decision making. Several types of leadership models were considered as explanatory of police officer decision making. Most seriously considered were models of situational leadership and the "impossible jobs" concept developed by Hargrove and Glidewell (1990) (Crothers and Vinzant 1994).

As the concept of street-level leadership began to take shape, it became apparent that it might have applicability to areas of public service beyond law enforcement. The researchers first explored the theoretical dimensions of that question (Vinzant and Crothers 1996). The empirical component of the study was then substantially expanded as well to include additional police officers, as well as a variety of other public employees in the social services.

The interaction between the theoretical and empirical aspects of this research was crucial to the development of the model of street-level leadership presented in Chapter Three. Concepts were refined and tested as the research evolved. As a consequence, the model of street-level leadership is firmly grounded in real-world situations and is, we argue, generally applicable to frontline public-service workers.

The Problems of Participant Observation

Since both the model of street-level leadership and the cases which inform and illustrate it were built from direct observations of frontline public servants, it is important to note and account for the weaknesses inherent in the participant-observation method. At least three problems, in particular, come to the forefront with this method: access to relevant agencies and actors to be observed; ethical issues derived from potential harm to subjects of research; and observer bias (Johnson and Joslyn 1986; West 1996; Hoffmann 1980; Lopata 1980; Johnson 1975; Jorgensen 1989; Sieber 1982). Answering each of these concerns is necessary if the results of the research are to be generally applicable.

Access
Gaining access to the various agencies and workers studied for this book was, in general, a comparatively easy task. As the description of the genesis of this book makes clear, the original access point was achieved spontaneously. Subsequently, research with other agencies was achieved by following procedures these organizations had either established or developed as the requests for research were made. Such procedures varied in their difficulty from making a simple phone call to an office supervisor who then received authorization from another supervisor, to making presentations to supervisors and workers in order to win their approval for the observations, to being required to get a court order to gain access to an agency (at the insistence of agency administrators, who wanted the court order for their own protection rather than to exclude the researchers from the agency). In these ways the

authors were able to gain access to every agency with which they desired to conduct research.

As for gaining access to relevant workers, since the research focused on line-level public servants, the choice was made to observe only workers who lacked supervisory responsibilities. In order to make each observation as complete as possible, a further decision was made to observe only those workers who usually dealt with clients on an interventionist, or temporary, basis. While workers might have multiple contacts with the same clients over time, this was a by-product of their work, not its main goal. Rather than following case managers or detectives, then, the decision was made to observe patrol officers and social-service workers/ investigators. Supervisors and workers were briefed about the general purposes of the study (to study how they made decisions in the field) and assured that their participation was voluntary and that their confidentiality as well as the confidentiality of their clients would be protected. In order to attempt to overcome any self-selection bias, the authors rode with workers as referred by shift supervisors, thereby observing a broad distribution of workers. In the case of social-service workers, the supervisors typically did so based on who had received an interesting or complicated referral that day and on a desire to have the observers ride with as many different workers as possible. Although participation was completely voluntary, virtually all were willing to allow the observers to accompany them. Many said they welcomed having the researchers ride along.

Ethics

In an effort to build trust with the workers with whom observations were conducted, the authors promised them absolute anonymity. Further, as part of the waivers the authors were required to sign before being allowed to conduct this research, they had to agree not to reveal the names of any clients. Accordingly, neither the names of the workers with whom observations were conducted nor those of the clients with whom they worked appear either in the authors' notes or in this text. Additionally, while each of the observations presented in this book is true and was witnessed by at least one of the authors, no details about where the observation took place are revealed. When necessary, details are left out or changed in order to prevent any identification of the incident with a particular agency, place, or person, thereby further protecting the anonymity of both clients and workers. It is for a similar reason that, when not referring to police officers or sheriff's deputies as "workers," the text refers to them generically as "officers." Social-service workers/investigators are similarly called "social-service workers" or in some cases "child protective services workers," regardless of their local titles.

The Hawthorne Effect

As a practical matter, the problems associated with reactive effects of observation, the so-called "Hawthorne effect," suffuses all participant observation. By being at a scene, in a car, in the area, or simply "around," the observer may encourage observed persons to change their behavior. There is, simply stated, no easy way to finesse the problem of observers influencing the behavior of those observed. This is particularly the case with police and social-welfare agencies, in part because it is difficult to gain access to files and information which may be used to confirm or negate observations. These agencies keep both their personnel and client records secret in order to protect confidentiality, legal rights, and similar values. So it is generally not possible to get access to a worker's personnel file and find, for example, that while the worker handled an observed case in a relatively nonbiased way, the individual had been cited for client abuse multiple times in the past. The potential remains, therefore, that the case was handled in a manner that was atypical for that worker.

The potential problems with observer bias in this research were addressed in several ways. First, many observations were conducted. Simply making multiple observations is a partial check on the observer-bias problem. Over time, it is unlikely that any individual or organization can consistently present a false face to an observer. This is particularly true when there are multiple observers and multiple environments—as was the case in this research. That is, the likelihood of an agency or individual "getting away with" misrepresenting their work diminishes as the number of observers, arenas of observation, and number of observations increase. To the degree that bias may be present in any case, it can be contextualized and made less significant if patterns emerge across cases and agencies.

Additionally, there were any number of times when observations occurred on an *ad hoc* basis. With police, in particular, it was common for an officer with whom an observation was being conducted to arrive, unannounced, on a scene a fellow officer was working. Usually, this was explained as giving the researcher the opportunity to see how other officers worked (and, it should be noted, was generally done only on slow nights). Under such circumstances, the presence of the observer *did* influence the behavior of the observed—and in such circumstances, the observations were discredited. However, such "accidental" observations did provide the researchers with an opportunity to check on the actions of *other* officers, *often without the other officer's knowledge*. Thus, if an author had or was scheduled to observe another officer, these informal observations served as a check on the problem of observer bias; similarities and differences could be noted and officer decisions could be evaluated in light of this knowledge.

The authors also carefully listened to the workers whom they were observing. This may seem like a small point, but it is in fact significant for a number of reasons. First, while an underlying assumption of the problem of observer bias is that subjects resent or are upset by the observation, and so shape their actions in reaction to imposed external norms, this did not usually appear to be the case with the workers observed for this book (excepting some workers who clearly were not supportive of the project or the observations). In general, workers appeared to enjoy the opportunity to share their ideas and experiences. The work they do, after all, is often solitary and cannot be fully comprehended by those who have not experienced it. Having someone to talk to, then, especially someone who was not part of the organization but who had at least some knowledge about the job, provided workers with an opportunity to explain their motives, attitudes, and so on. Importantly, there was substantial variation among workers along these dimensions, and, usually, the attitudes and values the workers expressed seemed to shape their actions. In those cases where a disjunction emerged between what workers said and what they did, the possibility of observer bias was highlighted.[4]

Listening to workers also provided the researchers with an opportunity to learn what they say about each other. As is the case

---

4. One could object that the converse is true: that when expressed attitudes and behaviors concur, observer bias is also present. This is hypothetically possible, and was checked by doing multiple observations and by listening to other workers talk about each other.

in any social situation, likes and dislikes, friendships and antago-
nisms, and respect or disrespect emerge among the individual
employees of an agency. Having a disinterested observer along—
particularly one who is sworn to secrecy—provided workers with
the opportunity to express their opinions and feelings about their
coworkers. While not all workers did this, many did. This provided
the researchers with yet another check on the problem of observer
bias. If multiple workers suggest that a coworker has real problems
in one area, and then an observation is conducted with that
coworker, any apparent disparity between others' opinions and the
events in the case at hand can highlight the issue of observer bias.

Additionally, it can be argued that the presence of an observer
is not, in these cases, unusual or artificial. Rather, the presence of
observers and bystanders is a fairly normal occurrence. As is noted
in Figure 1, the presence of witnesses, onlookers, etc., can be a factor that influences worker decision making. Nonetheless, the
observer's presence may have placed greater emphasis on the variable of onlookers than would have been the case were the observer
not present. But since the purpose of the research was to assess the
factors that influence workers' actions rather than to evaluate
workers' true motives, the problem can be argued to be relatively
minor. What really matters is whether workers respond appropriately to the matrix of influences they encounter, not whether one
variable was of greater significance than it might otherwise have
been. It is on this issue that the model of street-level leadership
developed in Chapter Three is focused.

Finally, the researchers also used their own judgments. In the
end, such research is a human enterprise—with all the risks that
the concept entails. If a worker who is broadly reported to be lazy
accuses other workers of interfering, for example, the authors used
their own judgments of whom, if anyone, to believe based on
what they observed.

The Cases: Agencies and Communities

It is not possible to make general claims unless the types of issues
and variables examined in the cases can be seen to mirror those in
multiple environments. In order to make this book as relevant as
possible, both the agencies that were studied and the general conditions in which they operated were selected to be as representative as possible.

Two primary types of agencies were used as the research focus for this book: police departments and social-service agencies. While these agencies and the workers who serve in them may seem radically different, in fact they share numerous qualities that make it useful to study them together. Workers in these agencies regularly deal directly with the public, independently perform duties that are varied and complex, and confront situations involving crisis and conflict. They often exercise a significant amount of discretion, but their choices are constrained by a complex set of factors. Finally, the legitimacy of the specific decisions made by workers in such agencies is a common source of controversy and contention.

Although a few observations were also conducted in mental health and emergency services, the majority of the observations were conducted in the following specific agencies: 1) Huntsville, AL, Police Department; 2) Spokane County, WA, Sheriff's Department; 3) Illinois Department of Children and Family Services, Bloomington, IL; and 4) Arizona Department of Economic Security, Phoenix, AZ. Only a brief description of these agencies and the environments in which they operate is provided here. More detailed descriptions of these organizations and the areas they serve is provided in the Appendix.

The Huntsville, AL, police department serves a midsized, economically and racially diverse southern city. The Patrol Division serves the city in three shifts of approximately sixty officers, who each patrol relatively small zones. Response times are relatively quick, and backup is usually readily available. In contrast, the Spokane, WA, Sheriff's Department serves a larger, more rural, and homogeneous area surrounding the City of Spokane (which has its own police department) in the Pacific Northwest. The eight to fourteen deputies who work the various shifts patrol much larger geographic areas than those working in Huntsville, making response times longer and backup less readily available. The Bloomington field office of the Illinois Department of Children and Family Services serves a very diverse three-county area encompassing both urban and rural populations in a midwestern state. Finally, the Phoenix area field offices of the Arizona Department of Economic Security serve the citizens of a large and growing metropolitan area of the Southwest.

The similarities and differences among these agencies make it possible to generalize from the insights generated in this research.

To the degree that differing economic, geographic, ethnic, and racial population variables shape what social-service workers do, the diversity of environments in which this research was conducted should encompass these influences in their many forms.

Shifts and Workers

The authors observed workers as they did their jobs, usually accompanying them for their entire shifts. With the police agencies, observations were conducted during all three patrol shifts and on every day of the week. Due to differences in call volumes and the significance of the incidents under investigation, 80 percent of all observations with police were conducted during second and third shifts, or from approximately 4:00 p.m. to 7:00 a.m. The remaining observations were conducted with day-shift patrols. With social-service workers, most observations were conducted as they worked their normal shifts, usually from 8:00 a.m. until 5:00 or 6:00 p.m. (or whenever the worker quit for the day, which in some cases was much later in the evening). A significant number of ride-alongs also occurred with after-hours and weekend crisis teams.

The research focus that directed these observations was relatively simple: the authors observed what workers did and listened to their explanation of why they did it. In some cases the sources of worker actions were obvious to both the worker and the observer—such as the case of the teenager in a red Ford Mustang told in Chapter Four. Additionally, as time allowed, workers were asked open-ended questions about their reasoning in making decisions. The authors also used their own judgments in deciding what variables influenced worker choice making and how these decisions could be evaluated.

Both authors observed both police officers and social-service workers on all shifts and in a wide variety of circumstances. The police research was largely conducted from the winter/spring of 1991 through the summer of 1993; the observations with social-service workers were mostly conducted from the summer of 1996 through the winter of 1997. Some days were intense and exciting; others were exceedingly dull. As one police officer described, many days were characterized by hours of sheer boredom interrupted by moments of stark terror. Indeed, many days brought no useful observations; others were filled with them.

The stories told and the observations made in this book are based on real situations faced by real workers. Moreover, different types of frontline workers were observed in a variety of situations, confronting varying types of problems in diverse locations and environments. Based on these and other factors, we assert that the stories told and the conclusions drawn in this book provide a useful and important perspective that can be used to understand street-level public service across a variety of programs, organizations, and communities.

Before this worker-centered perspective can be more fully developed, however, there are some key theoretical issues and dilemmas inherent in the work of street-level public servants that must be considered. Chapter Two explores these issues and examines the strengths and weaknesses of existing models of public service in light of these theoretical issues and the realities of frontline public service.

2

Discretion and Legitimacy in Frontline Public Service

The Work of Street-Level Public Servants: Just One Broken Bone

A child protective services (CPS) worker was on her way to the hospital. As she drove, she explained the background of the case she was investigating. Two days before, a nurse from a local doctor's office had called to report a four-month-old with a suspicious compression fracture of the femur (thigh bone). The police had responded to a domestic violence call at the parents' home the night before. The husband had reportedly kicked his wife off the bed to the floor. The police were investigating to determine whether he would be charged with felony assault and endangerment. When she called, the police had told the CPS worker that the man had a "long criminal history" including assault, domestic violence, and robbery. The police had not been aware, however, that the baby had been injured.

The CPS worker explained to the observer that she had already made an initial visit to the home to talk with the parents. Both were teenagers and lived with the paternal grandmother. The mother worked at a manufacturing plant. The father was unemployed and claimed that he could not get work because of his criminal record. He, along with the paternal grandmother, cared for the child while the mother worked.

When the CPS worker asked the parents how the baby had broken her leg, the father had said that his wife and

*baby had fallen off the bed. When the worker said she knew
about the domestic violence call to the police, he had
changed his story, saying that he pushed the mother off the
bed with his foot while she was nursing the baby and that
the baby "probably hurt her leg then." The worker had then
requested, and the mother agreed, that the baby be brought
to the hospital for a bone scan and exam to determine if
there were any prior injuries. The worker was able to sched-
ule the exam for two days later.*

*In the meantime, the CPS worker said she had checked
with the police again. The officer had told her that the
mother and baby had moved in with her mother. The husband had come to her mother's house and threatened her
and the police had been called. Subsequently, the mother
signed an order of protection (restraining order) against her
husband.*

*As she pulled into the parking lot of the hospital, the
worker commented that "with just one broken bone, the case
might not stick. I may have to close it. But first, I want to
check to see if anything else shows up on the bone scan. If it
does, then the picture changes."*

*When she arrived at the hospital, the worker was sur-
prised to find both parents and the baby in the waiting room.
The worker greeted the parents and thanked them for bring-
ing the baby. She then turned the infant seat around to check
on the baby. The baby, a pink-cheeked little girl, was alert
and did not appear to be in any immediate distress. The
mother was very thin and quiet. She slumped down in her
chair and did not make eye contact. The man, who was tall
and stocky, was friendly and polite. When the nurse called,
he offered to take the baby back to the examining room. The
CPS worker agreed.*

*After he left, the worker turned to the mother. She asked
why the father was present. "Don't you have a restraining
order?" she asked. The mother said, "Yes, but I thought he
should be here." The worker explained to her that it was very
important that she not voluntarily violate the protection
order if she wanted to avoid contact with her husband at
other times. She then told the mother that, under the circumstances, she didn't think it was a good idea for the baby to*

"go back to grandma's house for day care." She told her that the decision to move into her mother's house was probably a good one and offered to arrange and pay for alternative child care. The mother mumbled something about not having any support. She then said, "My mom doesn't want me living with her. She has her own problems." The worker again offered to arrange day care. The mother just looked at the floor.

At that point, the father returned with the baby. After he set down the baby seat, the worker asked to speak to him privately. They stepped out in the hallway and the worker said in an even tone, "I think you should leave. You are violating an order of protection." The father became angry. He yelled, "Who are you people? My parents?" The worker said calmly but firmly, "No. I am here to make sure your baby is safe." The father then became enraged. His face flushed red and he began shaking his fist. "What do you think? You think you can just take my kid? I'm taking her and getting out of here." The worker stepped in front of him, looked him in the eye, and said in a very clear and directive tone, "Yes, if you don't calm down I can take your child. If you do calm down, I'd be glad to answer any questions. But, you are not taking the baby with you now." He growled, shook his fist, swore loudly, and left.

The mother and the worker then took the baby in to the doctor's office for a complete exam. The doctor explained that the bone scan had showed no prior broken bones. She quizzed the mother about how she fell when her husband had pushed or kicked her off the bed. The mother explained that she had landed on her elbows and knees to protect the baby, and while the baby had hit the floor, she had not fallen on top of her. The doctor told her that the baby's current injury could not have been sustained by such a fall. The doctor said, "This injury resulted from considerable force, much more force than the incident you describe." The mother began to cry.

The worker again told the mother that she had to protect the baby by keeping her away from the people in the house where the injury occurred, or CPS would have to take temporary custody of her. The worker again offered to arrange for child care. The mother said that she and the baby could stay with friends and that the friends could "watch her while I work."

The worker then stepped outside the examining room and requested that the hospital's domestic violence counselor talk with the mother. The counselor and the mother talked while the CPS worker waited outside. Afterward, the worker walked the mother to her car. On the way, she again reminded her how important it was to not violate the restraining order and to not take the baby to the paternal grandmother's house for day care. The mother nodded. When arriving at the mother's car, the worker noticed that the rear view mirrors had been torn/knocked off and that the windshield had been broken in several places. She asked the mother how it happened. She simply said, "He did it."

As the worker walked to her car she said, "I hate cases like this. You have to hope for the best, and I don't."

INTRODUCTION

As was explained in Chapter One, street-level public servants often confront situations that are ambiguous, complicated, unpleasant, and sometimes even dangerous. In making decisions about how to handle these situations, there are multiple and sometimes competing variables which can influence their choices. In balancing these pressures, workers exercise discretion. A consideration of the legitimacy of these discretionary choices is necessary not only to improve the effectiveness of their choices, but also to fully understand worker discretion in the context of governance. It is the purpose of this chapter to explore these concepts and issues.

DISCRETION AND LEGITIMACY

At the heart of the matter of worker decision making is the concept of *discretion*. Some public servants, for complex and interactive reasons, have to exercise discretion as they do their jobs. In the case that introduces this chapter, for example, the worker exercised discretion in several ways. She decided whether or not to request that a bone scan be done on the baby, and in doing so made a decision about continuing the investigation. Doing so was an explicit decision to expend public funds for the investigation and the related costs of the medical exam and other services that may be offered/provided. She exercised discretion in determining whether to leave the baby in the parents' custody until the exam was completed. She also decided whether to confront the father about violating the restraining order, and if so, whether she would do it immediately or later. She made choices about how to deal with the father when he became angry at the hospital and threatened to take the baby. She made decisions about the approach she would use to talk to the mother and to try to convince her to stay away from the father. She had to determine whether she trusted the mother enough to send the baby home with her. Finally, she had to decide whether to close the case, keep it open, or to refer it to another unit for ongoing monitoring.

The legitimacy of the worker's choices may be questioned. The father, the mother, the grandmother, the worker's supervisor, the court, the media, and others might suggest that the worker should have done something other than what she did, based on their perception of the situation, their interests, their knowledge, and their values. In fact, it seems likely that if ordinary citizens were to hear that a case of child abuse might not be pursued because the baby had "just one broken bone," they might view the worker's failure to remove the child as illegitimate. Yet the worker's evaluation of the situation and interpretation of local laws and department rules and norms, based on her experience, suggested that her decision was legitimate according to those standards.

Thus, questions of legitimacy are inextricably bound with the issue of discretion, and both must be addressed if the nature and significance of street-level decision making is to be understood. In order to understand how discretion and legitimacy manifest themselves in the work of street-level public servants, it is necessary to examine each concept in some detail.

The Nature of Discretion

The exercise of bureaucratic discretion has been a central and enduring issue in the field of public administration. Questions about the scope of bureaucratic discretion, how and to what extent it should be controlled, and how it can be reconciled with the values of democratic governance have been and will continue to be debated. Most frequently, the issue of bureaucratic discretion has been approached from the standpoint of the role of executive branch agencies in the political system and the balance of power. In 1958, Sayre stated, "The responsibility and responsiveness of the administrative agencies . . . is of central importance in a government based increasingly on the exercise of discretionary power by the agencies of administration" (105). After all, as Morrow points out, politics is the struggle for control of policy. If administrative agencies possess policy-making power through the exercise of discretion, they become targets and participants in that political struggle (Morrow 1980).

Discretion is also an important issue, however, from the perspective of the individual street-level worker. What is the nature of discretion in this context? In simple form, discretion can be defined as "the ability to make responsible decisions," and "the power of free decision or latitude of choice within certain legal bounds" (Merriam–Webster, Inc. 1996). Although the dictionary is often an insufficient source for understanding (as opposed to defining) a concept, it turns out that these definitions provide a useful starting point for exploring a number of important dimensions of frontline worker discretion.

First, the preceding definition of discretion embodies the concept of *choice*. Discretionary acts involve making choices among alternatives. The decision maker has latitude in making choices in the sense that no one factor forces the selection of one alternative versus all others. It is the judgment of the choice maker, then, rather than some mechanistic process, that explains why one particular alternative is selected.

Second, the definition suggests that although the decision maker has latitude, discretion is *constrained* by external factors. Discretion is more than autonomous choice making; it involves making decisions within "certain legal bounds" or "responsible" criteria. While no factor may be causing a particular selection, the *range* of discretionary alternatives is bound by external variables. Choices are not made at will or with complete freedom. Rather, discretion is limited.

Third, the concept of discretion implies that there is (or may be) variation among the factors that constrain discretion. That is, the dictionary definition does not indicate that there are specific "legal bounds" or detailed criteria by which "responsible decisions" can be determined in all cases. Instead, there may be differences among individuals, groups, communities, agencies, clients, or other actors in a particular situation in terms of how they would define the constraints on discretion.

A fourth aspect of discretion offered here derives not from the dictionary definition, but from direct observations of street-level workers in action. Discretion manifests itself in two somewhat distinct dimensions: *process* (the means or how a goal is to be accomplished) and *outcome* (the ends or what goal is to be sought). As Barth points out, ". . . Serving the public interest in a democracy requires ongoing concern with not only what is done but also with how it is done" (1992, 289). While this distinction between process and outcomes is in one sense a highly artificial one, it can be an analytically useful way to think about the kinds of choices that street-level public servants are called upon to make (Crothers and Vinzant 1994; Vinzant and Crothers 1994).

It is, for example, sometimes necessary for workers to make decisions about *what* to do. There may be a range of options that can be seen as "responsible" or within "certain legal bounds" in a given situation, so the worker has to decide which outcome or objective to pursue. Such discretion is termed here *outcome* discretion.

Workers also are called upon to exercise discretion in deciding *how* to achieve a goal. In some cases, the outcome or objective to be sought may be required by law, routine, procedure, or some other factor, but there is a range of means by which the goal can be realized. Such discretion is termed here *process* discretion. Process and outcome discretion can be exercised singly or together. In other words, sometimes workers exercise both outcome and process discretion in the same situation when they must make choices about both *what* will be done and *how* it will be done.

Finally, the concept of discretion implies that the appropriateness or inappropriateness of the choices made can be evaluated. This evaluation can be based on constraints and/or outcomes. Since discretion, by definition, must be exercised within legal and other parameters, worker decisions can appropriately reflect these constraints or can transgress such boundaries and stray into illegality and/or irresponsibility. For example, a social-service worker may apply racist or sexist criteria to decide whether a child ought to be removed from a home, or a police officer may be more willing to arrest or use excessive force with members of a particular ethnic group. Such choices can be seen as abuses of discretion, of its use outside legal bounds or responsible criteria.

Alternatively, a worker may make an appropriate discretionary choice based on the constraints, and yet the case may go "wrong" in unforeseen ways. For example, an outwardly calm man with no prior history of violence may harm his wife as soon as the police leave. A police officer may allow a vehicle that meets some but not all of the criteria for a suspected drunk driver to pass by—and moments later that vehicle might be involved in a fatal accident. Based on the information available, a child protective services worker may choose not to remove a child from a potentially abusive home—and that child's parents may injure or even murder the child later that day. Outcomes, then, may be unsuccessful even if discretionary choices are appropriate with regard to the factors considered in arriving at the decision.

For example, one of the cases observed during this project involved a social-service worker who was called to investigate a report of suspected child abuse. A school official had called the local child-abuse hotline to report that a boy had come to school with bruises around his wrists, suggesting that he could have been tied up or otherwise inappropriately restrained. As is required under the law, the worker went to the school, interviewed the boy, and discovered that there were, in fact, bruises around his wrists.

As a part of the investigation, the worker then went to the boy's home to interview the parent(s). He found the mother at home. She responded to the worker openly and seemed cooperative. He explained that he was following up on a report of suspected abuse and that under the law, he was obliged to investigate. He asked the woman if she had seen the bruises, if she or someone in the home might have caused the bruises, or if she could account for them in any way. She had an immediate answer. She stated that the child, who both she and the worker said was "slow," was obsessive about a new wristwatch he had recently received. He would play with it throughout the school day. This angered his teacher, and in order to avoid playing with the watch, the boy would push it as far up his arm as it would go. This, the mother explained, accounted for the bruises.

After asking the mother which arm the boy wore his watch on—bruises were present on both arms—and receiving the answer "both," the worker thanked the woman, explained the department's procedures in this case, and indicated that he would report that no abuse had been committed. Later, in discussion with the observer, the worker noted that 90 percent of what he did in his job was decide abuse had *not* been committed. He said that in this case it was a judgment call that was based on his experience with children with developmental difficulties. Such children, he said, were likely to be obsessive about things like a wristwatch; thus he felt the mother's story was credible.

From another perspective, however, it is easy to see the many ways in which the discretion the worker exercised might be questioned or have "gone wrong." Most people, after all, wear a watch on only one arm; they might get bruises on one arm, but not both. The worker did not go back to the school to interview the teacher to verify the mother's story, nor did he reinterview the child about the watch. Moreover, the fact that the boy's playing with the watch had led to a report on the family might cause the boy to be severely punished. In other words, by investigating the case, the worker might *stimulate* abuse, and by closing the case, he had no legal right to check on the child in the future. It is also true, however, that if the worker had not closed the case, the time he spent following up on the mother's story would prevent him from proceeding with other investigations that may or may not have turned out to be more serious. Other possibilities surely exist. Only circumstances, and time, could tell.

In short, discretion is anything but simple. Discretion is constrained choice among competing alternatives; it may involve decisions about what to do, how to do it, or both; and its appropriateness and reasonableness can be evaluated. As such, discretion is a neutral concept in that it is neither good nor bad in and of itself. Instead, it is the context of its use that establishes its meaning and reasonableness.

Sources of Discretion in Street-Level Public Service

Why do many street-level public servants exercise discretion in their daily work? Why don't we, as a society, simply eliminate their discretion and thereby avoid the whole problem of having to determine whether it is reasonable or appropriate? Michael Lipsky's seminal work in *Street-Level Bureaucracy* (1980) explored this question. Workers such as police officers, social-service workers, and the like, Lipsky argued, *must* exercise discretion for several reasons.

First, discretion is required to apply rules in specific cases because "street-level bureaucrats often work in situations too complicated to reduce to programmatic formats" (Lipsky, 1980, p. 15).

It is, for example, impossible to establish objective criteria for exactly how much "weaving within a single lane" (a criterion that police officers may use to determine whether to stop a car for a DUI/DWI check) is *too* much. It might be a windy or rainy night; a vehicle may appear to have been in an accident recently and so its alignment may be out; or the driver may be intoxicated. Such decisions are, fundamentally, judgment calls that cannot follow predetermined bureaucratic routines.

Second, Lipsky suggested that some situations require public employees to make judgments about people: "Street-level bureaucrats work in situations that often require responses to the human dimensions of situations" (Lipsky 1980, 15). A social-service worker, for example, might be required to evaluate a parent's explanation for a child's bruises. The evidence may be unclear. Children do, after all, fall down; not every injury is abuse. Yet if an injury is the result of abuse, the child ought to be protected from further harm. The worker's choice about how to handle the situation is, at least in part, a judgment about the people with whom he or she is dealing. No formula can remove such judgments from the process.

Third, because "street-level discretion promotes workers' self-regard and encourages clients to believe that workers hold the key to their well-being," the practice of discretion is reinforced (Lipsky 1980, 15). In other words, workers need to feel they can make the decisions that are necessary for them to do their jobs. The kinds of problems many such workers deal with are often of the most depressing and intractable kind. Under such circumstances, some measure of individual control and choice gives workers a needed sense of empowerment to cope with the situations they confront. Additionally, as clients see workers exercise discretion, they understand that their fate is in some sense dependent on the worker's choices. As a result, clients are likely to support a worker having discretion, at least up to the point that it helps them. For example, both the client and the worker in an employment agency know that the worker has the ability to make the client's path to a job better and easier. This relationship becomes mutually reinforcing as the worker exercises discretion and the client wants the discretion exercised in his or her favor.

Finally, Lipsky noted that some public employees operate largely independently of direct supervision as they carry out their tasks (Lipsky 1980). For example, patrolling police officers may come upon a street fight. Under most circumstances, it is the officers on the scene who can best evaluate the situation and make a judgment about whether or not to place the participants under arrest. A supervisor cannot physically be present nor be called to the scene to oversee all such decisions. These are choices that must be made on the street by the officers present. Similarly, many social-service workers go to calls well away from the central office. It is necessary for workers to make a number of judgments about these cases—how to handle clients, what questions to ask, whether to request services or legal action—without supervisory assistance or review for the simple reason that the supervisor is not present and cannot see and hear what the worker sees and hears.

Put in the context of the case that introduces this chapter, Lipsky's conceptualization of the inevitability of discretion is descriptively accurate. The worker was at a scene far from immediate supervisor review. The situation had a number of factors—the presence and attitude of the father, the activities of the doctor, and so on—that made it unlikely that there would be any preestablished bureaucratic routine that could cover every contingency. The worker was faced with assessing both parents' reactions to the evidence and information they were confronting, thus requiring a reaction to the human dynamics of the situation. The mother wanted the worker to exercise her discretion in a way that overlooked the father's presence on the scene, thereby acting in the client's favor. Under such circumstances the worker's exercise of discretion, as Lipsky rightly suggested, was inevitable.

The Changing Nature and Scope of Discretion

Since the time that Lipsky's important insights were published, the context in which bureaucratic discretion is exercised and evaluated has changed. As a result of these changes, the scope and range of street-level discretion have significantly increased. Some of the pressures for increased discretion are organizational and managerial, some are political, some are based on changing public and community expectations, and some arise from the changing nature of the problems street-level workers confront.

At the organizational level, the nature and location of discretion are changing in response to the implementation of new management approaches. Public managers are responding to the exhortations in the management literature and from politicians to follow their private-sector counterparts in implementing management systems that empower individual workers, such as Total Quality Management, responsibility-centered management, and community-based programming. As the *Report of the National Performance Review* puts it, "empowering employees to get results" and shifting accountability "from inputs to results" (Gore 1994, 37–40) are the emerging management paradigm. In general, these management approaches emphasize decentralization, teamwork, ongoing improvement and attention to quality, and an emphasis on "customer" satisfaction—all of which push decision-making authority downward in the organization and accountability outward to the community. The emphasis is on getting results that will meet the needs of an agency's "customers," be they citizens, elected officials, the media, community leaders, interest groups, or governmental staff agencies. As the "reinvention permission slip" in the Department of Education reads, "You have the authority and responsibility to make government work better and cost less" (Gore 1994, 15). As a consequence of such new administrative and management systems, more and more agencies are placing discretion in the hands of the workers, who are expected to be innovative and responsive in meeting "customer" wants and demands. While the advisability and appropriateness of using this market metaphor in the public sector is debatable (Carroll 1995; Fox 1996; Frederickson 1996), few would deny its current significance.

The political environment of governmental service has changed as well. Antigovernment sentiments have reached an almost fevered pitch. It has become a truism in the minds of many Americans that the government is completely mismanaged. This is particularly reinforced by the increasingly adversarial relationship the media has with government institutions—newspaper, magazine, and television reports are regularly filled with a chronicle of agency failures. This antigovernment mood creates new and sometimes conflicting pressures on public agencies with regard to the exercise of discretion. In one sense, the overall antibureaucracy mood and the desire to decrease the size and reach of the government cause some to think that the bureaucracy should exercise less discretion and be less involved with policy. At the same time, however, the *failure* to exercise discretion in a manner which meets community needs or improves management practice invites political and media scrutiny. In all cases, the legitimacy of discretionary choices can be under serious challenge.

Still other pressures for increased discretion are related to changing expectations and demands from both community groups and individual citizens. Citizens are increasingly demanding that local governments, schools, police departments, and other service agencies respond directly to neighborhood needs and demands. Individual police officers, social-service workers, and other public employees are expected to work with citizens in identifying and solving community problems. Individuals who interact with public employees, be they criminals, victims, clients, witnesses, or applicants, have generally become more demanding and less tolerant of bureaucratic rigidity. This requires that workers be given the latitude to tailor their responses to the situation at hand and to make different decisions in different contexts.

Finally, the nature and scope of discretion are changing in response to the increasing difficulty and complexity of the problems confronted by street-level workers. As Harmon and Mayer (1986) suggest, the tame, malleable problems that public servants were once hired to deal with, such as building roads and sewage systems, are largely solved. Instead, public servants are being asked to solve "wicked" problems. Wicked problems are problems with no solutions, no agreed-upon definitions, and no tests to measure the efficacy of programs intended to deal with them. Poverty, unemployment, homelessness, drug abuse, crime, and family decay are all examples of wicked problems. In each case, the problem is subject to multiple definitions and is treatable by no known, acceptable solution.

In the case of homelessness, for example, there are irreconcilable differences in beliefs about how the problem is defined, what causes it, and therefore, how it ought to be addressed. It has been suggested, for example, that homelessness arises from vagrancy, mental illness, income inequities, the lack of low-income housing, laziness, drug and alcohol abuse, and/or lack of moral character. Moreover, depending upon whether the individuals on the street are defined as drug addicts, hoboes, victims, vagrants, or bums, different public policies will be put in place to address the issue. None of these public policies are known to eliminate the problem, and each generally has negative repercussions which must be dealt with. In other words, public problems have become increasingly wicked in the sense that attempted solutions can become part of the problem and each new attempt seems to bring a new and vexing set of difficulties and social consequences.

Most importantly for the discussion here, "because of their uniqueness, wicked problems are not amenable to standardized routines for analysis and evaluation" (Harmon and Mayer 1986, 11). Consequently, wicked problems demand that frontline public employees exercise increasing amounts of discretion. They must exercise this discretion knowing that they are responsible for the social consequences of their actions, even when those consequences are unknown and unpredictable. Moreover, while the consequences are unknown, there are often, if not usually, some negative effects of public actions taken to solve wicked problems. Charting their way among the many difficult issues they may face requires that workers exercise significant discretion in the course of doing their jobs.

At a less abstract level, what "wicked" problems mean for street-level public servants can be seen in a case of reported child neglect. A worker from a weekend crisis team responded to a call from the police that a homeless woman had left her infant and toddler sitting alone on the edge of a busy street that summer afternoon while she went down the street asking for money. As it turned out, the woman was known to the agency. She had been investigated previously for child neglect and had been told by the last worker that if she could not provide a safe environment for her children, the agency would have to place them in foster care. Although the woman had promised to do so, this report indicated that she had not. The report said that the woman had been staying off and on at a local shelter, that she had been abused by her husband (who was also at the shelter intermittently), that she had drug and alcohol problems and a history of violence, and that the agency had referred her several times for mental health services, but that she had not cooperated.

The worker decided to ask for police escort and go to the shelter to take the children into custody for the remainder of the weekend. She would leave it to the regular (weekday) worker who had done the previous investigations to determine whether longer-term custody would be sought through the courts. When the woman and children were found at the shelter at around midnight, the woman simply said, "I know why you're here." The children, ages three years and six months, were awake, severely sunburned, and the older child appeared to have the flu or a bad cold. The children showed no emotion, however, and went willingly with the worker and the police. The worker left with the children to take them to another shelter for the night. As the worker and police left, the woman left the shelter and wandered into the night.

Such is the nature of "wicked" problems at the street level. Street-level problems, even wicked ones, do not often present themselves in neat and tidy isolation. Instead, they are often layered and tangled together in an almost incomprehensible bundle. Solving any one of these problems in these cases would be difficult at best; taken together, they are virtually unmanageable. No prearranged departmental rules can provide much guidance for action in these circumstances. The best a worker can do is evaluate the circumstances at hand and make judgments.

Whatever a worker decides to do, it will often not be enough to solve the immediate problem, much less the other issues and problems that might be part of the overall picture. Further, workers cannot be sure what the consequences of their decisions will be, not only in terms of addressing the immediate situation, but also in terms of the potential effect on the other problems that may be involved in a particular situation. In the case of the homeless woman, would the woman be beaten by her husband for losing the children? Would she become the victim of a crime as she wandered the dark streets? Would she take an overdose of drugs? Would the regular social-service worker take action to place the children in foster care or would she (or the judge) return the children to the mother? What would be the effect on the children in either case? Would the children be safe in the shelter for the night? Which piece of the puzzle could change the picture? If the mother could be convinced to get mental health treatment, could she then provide for her children? Or was her drug problem the primary barrier to adequate parenting? Would arranging for housing make a difference? There are certainly no clear-cut answers to these questions, and in some sense, there are no answers at all.

Cumulatively, these layered and tangled "wicked" problems, coupled with the organizational and political changes described earlier, conspire to make the exercise of discretion an inevitable, difficult, and very complicated part of the work that many frontline public servants do. These factors mean that there is an expanded range of decisions, an increased complexity in the decision-making process, and a heightened importance placed on how discretionary choices are judged in a larger context. Put simply, public servants are being asked to make more decisions, based on more factors, in more complicated situations—making discretion both more necessary and more important as they do their daily work.

Evaluating the Exercise of Discretion

As the opportunity and need to exercise discretion have increased in the last several decades, so too has the potential for multiple sources of challenge to worker decisions. As is suggested by Figure 1 in Chapter One, there may be many variables that influence the decisions that line-level public servants make. Indeed, it is, in part, because there are so many factors that can be considered that workers must exercise discretion in the first place. However, each of the individuals, groups, or institutions involved may judge worker choices differently.

For example, as the story about the baby with the broken bone that begins this chapter suggests, it is likely that different individuals would have separate and often inconsistent evaluative criteria for judging worker discretion. The pediatrician's nurse who made the report, the police officer who responded to the domestic violence call, the mother, the father, the grandmother, the doctor at the hospital, and the domestic violence counselor probably would have different ideas about what had happened and what should happen next. Certainly the father thought the mother's request that he follow the restraining order's requirements was improper. Similarly, the mother did not think that the order ought to apply in the specific case of the father's presence at the doctor's appointment. In addition to the participants, other key actors and organizations might impose differing constraints and values. The court, for example, might have viewed a request for a temporary custody order as unwarranted. Given the volume of new reports, the worker's supervisor might feel that the worker was getting too involved in a case where there was no clear evidence about who might have hurt the baby (the father may have done so, but so might the grandmother, the uncle who also spent a considerable amount of time in the house, or even the mother herself). In contrast, many citizens might expect that workers in such situations would take action to guarantee that no further injury to the child would occur, but at the same time they might decry the intervention of government workers into "family matters." Moreover, if the child were to sustain further and more serious injuries, the decisions of the worker would likely be questioned in the media. The possible iterations are almost endless. At the center of it all, individual workers have to make specific decisions in particular cases, each of which may be challenged or legitimated on multiple and competing grounds.

As will be seen throughout this book, competing visions of the appropriateness of choices like those that faced the child protective services worker are often present in the circumstances and cases that street-level public servants encounter. Almost inevitably, different interested parties will desire alternate outcomes and will judge the worker's choices in light of those preferences. Indeed, as is shown in Akira Kurasawa's classic film *Rashomon* (1951), it is often true that participants in the same case will have different recollections of what occurred—and thus will have different visions of what should have been done. Such competing expectations will almost inevitably complicate a worker's decision making. Extended throughout all the variables summarized in Figure 1 of the preceding chapter, with all the potential direct and indirect influences and interactions, evaluating the appropriateness of individual worker discretionary choices can seem daunting. Clearly, the matrix of influences that shape what workers do presents a constellation of competing and contentious standards. Yet regardless of how daunting the task may seem, workers are expected and required to make reasonable, effective choices in these contexts.

The Nature of Legitimacy

The varied and contentious interpretations of the appropriateness of worker actions that might arise in the course of the work street-level public servants do are, in the end, disputes about the *legitimacy* of worker choice making. Legitimacy is a concept that can be applied to both political regimes and political leaders, to institutions, and to individual actions. Shafritz defines legitimacy as "a characteristic of a social institution . . . whereby it has both a legal and a perceived right to make binding decisions" (1988, 324). Similarly, Jackman suggests that legitimacy "reflects the degree to which those who seek to rule (i.e., to exercise power) are accepted by the ruled. It thus identifies the nature of the relationship between rulers and ruled" (1993, 95). Put another way, legitimacy is the answer to the question posed by Geertz, "Who are you that I should obey you?" (1977, 251).

Like discretion, the concept of legitimacy is complex. At least part of the reason that the term "legitimacy" is problematic is that its literal definition is deceptively simple. The dictionary defines legitimacy as "accordant with law or with established traditions" and "conforming to recognized principles or accepted rules and standards" (Merriam–Webster, Inc. 1996). At first glance, such a definition seems to depart little from the notion of simple compliance. But when one considers the fact that workers (and the leaders of political regimes, for that matter) may be asked to make choices that are in accord or compliance with multiple and sometimes conflicting norms, laws, values, and rules, the more complex nature of legitimacy becomes apparent.

In order to apply the concept of legitimacy to an individual street-level worker's decisions, there are several aspects of the concept that must be defined and developed more fully. First, the concept of legitimacy assumes that there are external standards against which specific actions or behaviors are evaluated. That is, rather than being legitimate in and of itself, a particular decision or action derives its legitimacy from some outside source—i.e., tradition, following established procedures, reflecting shared values, and so on. In other words, legitimacy is contingent on the norms and values particular to the circumstance where it is being asserted, denied, or tested (Jackman 1993).

Second, legitimacy can be established based on any number of different criteria. For example, legitimacy may be established based on procedural grounds; the fact that a law was passed through well-established procedures in the legislative process may afford it legitimacy. Similarly, if a worker follows traditional practices in a specific type of case, these procedural norms may help to establish the legitimacy of the worker's choices. It is also possible to judge the legitimacy of a decision based on the outcomes or consequences of that decision. Other things being equal, if a decision or choice results in desirable consequences, its legitimacy is sometimes inferred. In other words, if a decision "works" in achieving a desirable outcome without violating other standards, the legitimacy of that decision will probably not be questioned. This echoes what Morgan (1990), drawing from the debate over the proper exercise of judicial discretion, describes as the process-oriented and results-oriented approaches to administrative legitimacy.

In short, there are multiple grounds, both procedural and substantive, upon which the legitimacy of decisions, behaviors, and institutions can be established. Conversely, there are many criteria by which legitimacy can be challenged. A law passed through democratic institutions, for example, may be procedurally legitimate, but if it reestablished slavery in the United States its legitimacy should and would be questioned on substantive, moral grounds. Similarly, if following traditional practices means ignoring the voice of a female spousal abuse victim in favor of the "head of the household's" word, then it would be reasonable to argue that the decision was inappropriate or illegitimate. Legitimacy, in this sense, is dynamic: it is established in context, and where the context changes, so does legitimacy.

Further, legitimacy is not an all-or-nothing concept (Jackman 1993). Because different people may have varying perspectives about which values, norms, and outcomes ought to be emphasized in a specific context, they will frequently disagree about questions of legitimacy. Because of these differing judgments, on balance, a decision or institution or process can be seen as *more or less* legitimate, considering these different views. Put simply, legitimacy is rarely a simple dichotomous, either/or, question. Instead, as Jackman puts it, legitimacy will most likely be a *relative* concept: "Legitimacy . . . simply requires a degree of acquiescence, an acceptance of the political order as generally reasonable, given the known or feasible alternatives" (Jackman 1993, 99).

Within this framework, a significant amount of important scholarly work has examined the concepts of legitimacy and discretion in public administration. For example, it has been argued that legitimate administrative discretion should be seen as a matter of constitutional principle (Rohr 1986), conservatorship (Terry 1990), morality and ethics (Lovrich 1981; Jos 1990), personal responsibility (Harmon 1990), stewardship (Kass 1990), practical wisdom or phronesis (Morgan 1990), citizenship (Cooper 1991), a means to check the power of politicians (Spicer 1990; Spicer and Terry 1993), and even potential heroism (Bellavita 1991).

While each of these perspectives is important, the work of Morgan (1990), Kass (1990), and Terry (1990) is of particular interest here because of their treatment of the normative dimensions of administrative discretion. Morgan suggests that the legitimate exercise of discretion by public administrators should be based on practical wisdom or "phronesis." Phronesis, he says, is "the capacity to conjoin knowledge of the principles of right action with considerations of what is suitable . . . in a world of particulars and variability" (Morgan 1990, 74). This capacity for phronesis, he argues, will enable administrators to exercise discretion in a way that is workable, acceptable, and "fitting" in terms of constitutional values and principles—or in other words, legitimate.

Kass (1990) contends that the legitimacy of the role of public administrators in the governance process must be based on the concept of stewardship. Stewardship is "the administrator's willingness and ability to earn the public trust by being an effective and ethical agent in carrying out the republic's business" (1990, 113). In this model, public administrators act as agents on behalf of the shared interests of society as embodied by the state. A steward is an agent who acts in a way that is both effective and consistent with ethical norms, "even when it is extremely difficult to reconcile and effectuate them" (117). By being good stewards, Kass says, public organizations and public administrators can both enhance their own legitimacy and protect the legitimacy of the governance process as a whole.

Terry (1990) takes a slightly different approach. He asserts that public administrators play a legitimate leadership role in governing, but that it should be a special type of leadership which he calls "administrative conservatorship." As administrative conservators, Terry argues that public administrators should both serve the public and preserve the distinctive competence and integrity of their organizations. They exercise authority, he says, which is grounded in the beliefs, values, and interest of the community they serve.

Together, the perspectives advanced by Morgan, Kass, and Terry highlight three important facets of legitimacy in public administration. First, legitimacy involves both what works and what is right. Second, legitimacy is inextricably tied to service to the public and public values. Third, in exercising legitimate discretion, public administrators act on behalf of organizations and institutions, not as independent decision makers.

But how do these perspectives apply to frontline workers? Although these perspectives provide an important framework, they do not speak directly to the exercise of legitimate discretion at the street level. Rather, they focus on public executives and administrative-level decision making. Moreover, these conceptions do not offer a model for assessing the legitimacy of street-level choices on a case-by-case basis. In other words, each of these conceptions offers important perspectives on the roles, responsibilities, and expectations of public administrators in American governance. In exercising discretion, public administrators *are* expected to be practical, wise, and responsible in their roles as stewards, conservators, citizens, moral actors, and even heroes within a constitutional context. Accordingly, they *do* play an important and legitimate role in governance. But so do frontline workers. *How do these public servants translate these roles and expectations into legitimate street-level action?* Just as Terry (1990) suggests that public executives must exercise a special form of leadership, we suggest that frontline employees must also exercise a special form of leadership that we call street-level leadership. As is explored more fully in Chapters Three and Four, this street-level leadership is exercised within a complex organizational, community, and political environment that is at least somewhat unique to frontline public service.

As such, in understanding the challenges and difficulties of legitimate street-level action, an understanding of the nature of that environment is critical. Just as the legitimacy of the field of public administration "rests on the legitimacy of the political community itself and the administrators' ability to serve and represent that community" (Kass 1990, 12), legitimacy of frontline public service is inextricably tied to the context in which discretion is exercised. In those cases where community support for a worker's agency is strong, standards are clear and values are broadly shared, *and* a worker's decisions and actions are judged to reflect those values and standards appropriately, establishing the legitimacy of those actions is relatively easy. However, where community support is absent, or standards and values are in contention, legitimate action is more difficult to determine and can more easily be challenged. In many cases, public-service work at the street level involves this latter type of decision-making environment. As such, whatever workers decide to do, some set of values may be violated and the legitimacy of their actions can often be questioned. *Therefore, in assessing the relative legitimacy of alternative courses of street-level action, it is important to carefully consider the nature of the situation and the decision-making context that the worker confronts.*

Take, for example, one of the situations observed for this book. One of the authors was with a police officer in a patrol car late one night when the officer saw a white man driving slowly the wrong way down a one-way street between two groups of African-American men in a low-income housing project. The white man was driving an expensive, new sport utility vehicle (SUV). The police officer who was observing this situation explained that since the man was driving such an expensive vehicle, he probably did not live in the project. Further, he said that the slow speed at which he was driving suggested either that he wanted something from the men—i.e., drugs—or that he had some other purpose in mind. Additionally, he explained, the complex was subject under federal law to a curfew in which nonresidents were not allowed on the property's grounds after 11:00 p.m. (it was after midnight at the time). Yet, other than driving the wrong way down a narrow residential street, the man was doing nothing "wrong." The officer, then, might have simply ignored the situation, might have stopped the SUV to ticket it for driving the wrong way, or any of a number of alternatives. Thus, when the officer stopped the man and said that he thought the man was trying to buy drugs, it is reasonable to question the legitimacy of this discretionary action: the officer was making several racial- and class-based assumptions about where the man lived, what his purpose was, what the African-American men were doing standing outside late at night, and so on. On the other hand, the particular housing project in which this incident took place was well-known in both the community and the police department as a drug-dealing area; the law required that residents of the complex be able to prove their residency so that the curfew could be enforced; and, more generally, society desires that the drug trade be controlled if possible. Depending on what values one emphasizes, then, the officer's choices could be questioned regardless of what actions he took.

Cumulatively, these many dimensions of legitimacy suggest that legitimacy can be contingent upon the relationship between a particular act, decision, policy, or behavior and the standards by which it is evaluated. Since there are multiple standards by which legitimacy can be both established and challenged, it is dynamic and subject to change, reinterpretation, reassertion, or all three at the same time. Legitimacy, in this sense, is *political*, meaning that it is constructed from the relationship of specific acts and particular evaluative standards. It is also political in a broader sense, in that it involves questions about the relationship between workers, the institutions they represent, and the public and governance process as a whole.

Discretion and legitimacy, then, must be considered together. Discretionary acts inevitably open themselves up to questions about appropriateness. The legitimacy of discretionary choices must be established through reference to the external norms, values, and ideals that shape the context in which specific decisions are made. Accordingly, when evaluating and describing the work done by individuals who exercise discretion, it is necessary to have a model that can encompass questions of both discretion and legitimacy in a particular context.

EXISTING MODELS OF PUBLIC SERVICE

Before presenting a new model of public service to reflect the realities of discretion and legitimacy at the street level, it is important to examine how well existing models of public service account for these factors. How do these models view discretion? What are the strengths and weaknesses of these models in understanding the contemporary context of street-level public service?

Traditionally, the issues of bureaucratic discretion and legitimacy have been understood through one or more of six theoretical lenses, each suggesting a different set of roles and responsibilities for public employees. These theoretical perspectives view frontline workers as bureaucrats, policy makers, power wielders, professionals, problem solvers, and/or political actors.[1] The following sections consider the strengths and weaknesses of each of these six models.

Model 1: The Bureaucrat

When writers like Woodrow Wilson and Frank Goodnow first attempted to define the role of public administrators at the turn of the century, their thinking was based on formal organization theory and a strict separation between politics and administration. Bureaucrats were deemed responsible for the efficient and politically neutral execution of the public will, as defined by elected

---

1. While these models provide a workable and useful framework for the analysis, it is recognized that the use of only six models may serve to oversimplify the literature on bureaucratic discretion and accountability. For example, Downs's (1967) model of bureaucratic self-interest could have been included as a seventh model. It was decided that to do so would not add substantial insight to the analysis.

officials. Wilson wrote, "[P]olicy will have no taint of officialism about it. It will not be the creation of permanent officials, but of statesmen whose responsibility to public opinion will be direct and inevitable" (Wilson 1887, 22). Likewise, Goodnow defined politics as the "expression of the will of the state," with administration serving a subordinate role in executing that will (Goodnow 1900, 28). As such, in this model discretion was not really an issue. Politicians were expected to make decisions while bureaucrats carried them out.

This view of public employees as neutral experts was consistent with Weber's (1946) description of bureaucracy as an organization that would achieve predictability and control through a hierarchical ordering of authority relationships, merit-based employment, rules and procedures, and the maintenance of records. Weber emphasized the advantages of the bureaucratic form for democratic systems in terms of speed, efficiency, neutrality, and consistent application of laws. Legitimacy, then, was not a problem workers would face, since their actions were undertaken in accordance with principles and rules established by elected and other accountable officials.

Applied to the case that begins this chapter, for example, the worker's actions should have embodied a straightforward application of the law and agency rules. Taken in pure form, the bureaucratic model suggests that the worker should have been able to evaluate the condition of the child, the capacities of the parents, and similar factors in relation to a set of specific criteria and standards which would be formally stated in writing. The decision as to whether she should return custody to the parents or retain it for the state, then, would not be hers to make. It would be based on whether doing so, or not doing so, was in accordance with the rules. Legitimacy, in this case, would be established solely on whether the department's rules were followed. Alternatively, if the agency lacked comprehensive rules to cover such a case, rules would need to be developed, or the case would have to be recategorized so as to fit the rules. The worker in this model is more akin to a clerk than an independent actor; the decision-making authority lies with the agency's rules.

While the wide-ranging ramifications of the bureaucratic form are important, the most pertinent question for the purpose here is: What are the strengths and weaknesses of the bureaucratic model in describing contemporary practice in street-level public service?

One way to answer this question is by considering whether the role of public employees in contemporary governance could be understood without reference to this model. It is clear that it cannot. Virtually all large, public organizations have bureaucratic characteristics. Moreover, the bureaucratic values of efficiency and neutrality remain critically important both within the field of public administration and in the expectations of citizens and their elected representatives; thus, to some degree street-level public servants are expected to act as neutral experts in the administration of public policies.

The problem with the bureaucratic model is that it cannot easily accommodate the exercise of discretion by public servants. It is, in fact, essentially impossible to imagine the model's usefulness in describing the cases that introduce both Chapters One and Two. The model, in effect, eliminates the worker as a decision maker—which, as the stories and accompanying theoretical discussions illustrate, is simply wrong. Thus, the bureaucratic view of the role of public servants is important in highlighting the continuing importance of orthodox values and the extent to which bureaucratic discretion is limited by these public expectations. The model, however, offers relatively little in terms of describing how these values can be reconciled with the need to exercise the level of discretion called for at present.

Model 2: Implementers and Policy Makers

Another way to understand the role of public employees in the democratic system is through the lens of policy implementation. Early writers in the area of policy implementation relied heavily on the bureaucratic view of organizations and suggested that the role of public administration consisted of the efficient implementation of politically determined goals. Later works, however, portrayed the implementation process as much more complex and multifaceted.

The self-conscious study of policy implementation is often said to have begun with the analysis by Pressman and Wildavsky (1973) of the failed implementation of a federal employment program in Oakland, California. Since that time, implementation theory has evolved with regard to the assumed nature of the policy process and the role of the public administrator in that process. Early research on implementation, including the work of Pressman and Wildavsky, assumed a top–down, linear policy process which was driven by the language of the statute and the intent of elected officials. The top–down model was predicated on the assumption that policy directives ought to be translated into program activities with as little deviation as possible. As such, policy makers made the only important decisions; street-level actors served only to follow the "correct" implementation process or thwart it by making changes.

Because of criticisms of this top–down approach, a number of bottom–up models were developed. As noted earlier, for example, Lipsky described how the decisions of street-level bureaucrats define public policy in many spheres. Similarly, Linders and Peters (1987) also suggested that, for successful implementation, program design must consider the needs and values of the implementers. In general, bottom–up models assumed the existence of a network of actors whose goals and actions must be considered in understanding implementation. In this model, those responsible for implementation often play a positive, necessary, and appropriate role in redefining and refocusing policy in light of line-level realities.

The third type of policy implementation model attempted to meld these top–down and bottom–up models. In the integrated model, implementation is seen as occurring in a circular policy process. For example, Nakamura (1988) argued that, instead of a linear process, implementation activities were a part of a seamless, interactive whole. From this perspective, adaptation and discretion in the implementation process are seen as necessary and desirable.

Again applied in the case that heads this chapter, implementation models would suggest different standards for legitimacy, depending on the type of model used. In a top–down model, which is more akin to the bureaucratic model, any deviation from the enacted policy would be seen as illegitimate. In a bottom–up model, if the agency lacked clear rules, any decisions she made could be seen as reasonable adaptations to the circumstances at hand.

The strength of these models lies in their ability to explain the importance of decision making by those charged with the implementation of public policy and the significance of their choices for policy outcomes. The problem with implementation models is that they either fail to recognize the inevitability of discretion or fail to offer guidance to evaluate its legitimacy. Discretion is either considered illegitimate (in top–down models), legitimate as such (in bottom–up models), or simply a reality that should be recognized. Accordingly, the policy maker/implementer model provides, at best, only a partial accounting for the issues of discretion and legitimacy that arise in the work of street-level public servants.

Model 3: The Power Wielder

The role of frontline public servants has also been described within the framework of power. In fact, one of the most common theoretical perspectives for the study of police behavior is based on the concept of power (Skolnick and Fyfe 1993).

Power is a highly useful concept in understanding police behavior, particularly in a traditional department. Officer choice making can be characterized by the use of more or less coercive power or force to achieve some desired end. Taking a suspect into custody, defusing a dispute, or securing public order, for example, may require differing amounts of coercion.

Power may also be important in understanding street-level public service in other areas as well. Certainly child protective services workers exercise power in taking children away from their parents. Mental health workers exercise power in restraining or retaining a patient without his or her consent. Power is exercised by these individuals, sometimes coercively.

One example of a model of police behavior that relies heavily on the notion of power was developed by Muir (1977). Muir argued that police–community interactions are "extortionate transactions" in which police monopolize the exercise of power in relation to subject behavior. Police actions are, Muir said, a product of officer views of human nature and their ability to integrate the use of necessary force into their outlooks on life. Patterns of supervision and law may shape these interactions, Muir continued, but it is the particular relationship between an individual officer and a particular subject that largely determines the exercise of discretion in particular cases.

From a power perspective, then, the worker whose case introduces this chapter would be seen as simply exercising the power she had as an agency employee. Her decision, then, would be based on her personal ideals, values, and expectations. Since the parents were found lacking by her standards, she employed her power to achieve her goal.

The concept of power and coercion in the context of contemporary public service, however, may be insufficient to describe the breadth and depth of responsibilities and discretion exercised by street-level workers. For example, some have suggested that police officers should be adept at cooperative, proactive approaches to community problem solving (Brown 1989; Pugh 1986; Friedmann 1992). Additionally, social-service workers are expected to counsel, educate, and support clients, not simply exercise power over them. Such interactions presume two-way communication and consideration of others. The use of unilateral power under such circumstances, even as a means of conflict resolution, is often not seen as desirable. Increasingly, workers are expected to defuse conflict and redirect clients and citizens rather than coerce or control them.

There is another, deeper theoretical problem with using power as the sole lens for viewing street-level discretion. Power, by itself, is an amoral concept. Power is simply a means to an end—it can be used as a means to achieve desirable or undesirable goals. But public employees work within a system of laws, moral standards, and community values aimed at the realization of larger public purposes, not just the use of force. Such norms and values are central to understanding the workers' roles and responsibilities. Consequently, power provides insufficient guidance for defining and understanding questions of legitimacy and discretion in street-level public service.

Model 4: The Professional

A fourth way to understand worker discretion and legitimacy is by relying on the concept of professionalism. Numerous authors have pointed to the importance of professionalism in controlling and influencing the choices of public servants. Mosher (1968), for example, argued that professionalism in public service is essential in managing the tension between unelected bureaucrats and the democratic process. Professional values are asserted to hold the legitimating principles that ensure democratic control over worker discretion. It is for this reason that professionalism in public service has even been described as democracy's "greatest hope."

Kearney and Sinha (1988) suggested that professionalism provides the critical bridge between science and politics in the democratic process. Workers acting as professionals can exercise discretion within the norms and values of their profession. Indeed, research has shown that in at least some areas of public service, professionalism was a more significant predictor of behavior than bureaucratic factors (Hodges and Durant 1989).

Within a professional approach to street-level public service, then, the social-service worker who was dealing with the baby with the broken leg at the beginning of the chapter would have used the values innate to her profession in determining what to do. As a professional social worker, professional norms may have led her to place protection of the child from a potentially abusive situation above the law that required her to keep families together whenever possible. Within the professional model, the legitimacy of the worker's decisions would be primarily related to the norms of her profession as a social worker.

There are several problems, however, with relying solely on the notion of professionalism as the standard by which the exercise of discretion is judged. The first and most basic problem is determining to which profession public servants belong. Nurses, teachers, social workers, and police officers, for example, all have their own professions with differing standards. It has been argued that public administration has itself become a profession as well. This makes the relative influence of socialization in both a specific service area and as a public employee somewhat unclear.

The literature in law enforcement and social services is replete with references such as "professionalized police force" and the "profession of social work." But there is also ongoing debate about what the term "professional" means and if it is even applicable to these types of jobs. In social work, for example, there has been a debate about who should be included in the profession (Popple 1995). Others ask whether social workers have sufficient autonomy to constitute a profession (Toren 1975; Hopps and Collins 1995). Another way to express the latter is whether the profession, by itself, is adequate to explain the behavior of social-service workers in practice, given the bureaucratic and other influences on their behavior. It appears not.

Even within the profession of public administration, there is no consensus on which values should be emphasized. Newland (1980), for example, argues that public administrators should commit to democratic ideals and constitutional values as their ethical base and guide to action. In contrast, Lipsky (1980) argues that professionalism should emphasize idealism, client autonomy, and a commitment to social change. Still another perspective is offered by Green, Keller, and Wamsley (1993), who suggest that professionalism in public administration should be based on political foundations and that it demands normative, constitutional, and rhetorical competence.

Finally, the value of professionalism in addressing the inherent tension between bureaucratic discretion and democracy is limited to the extent that professionals are accountable only to peers and their norms are resistant to change (Lipsky 1980). In short, while professionalism is an important force in influencing the exercise of discretion, it is an incomplete model to explain discretion, accountability, and responsiveness in the larger context of democratic governance and politics.

Model 5: The Problem Solver

Still another theoretical frame for understanding the behavior and legitimate role of public servants is based on decision-making theory. This perspective is particularly visible in the contemporary literature on law enforcement and social work. Goldstein (1990), for example, drew heavily from decision-making theory in building his model of problem-oriented policing. He based his conception on the logical progression of the rational decision-making model from identifying and defining the problem, developing and analyzing alternatives, choosing and implementing a strategy, and then evaluating its effectiveness. In other words, he suggested that rather than merely handle incidents, officers should systematically analyze the underlying community problems and devise strategies to address them.

In rough outline, modeling police as problem solvers means that police officers act as practical social scientists. Officers enter a community, study the problems that afflict it, develop programs aimed at alleviating the problem, and then implement and evaluate those plans in specific communities. In particular, police are expected to: 1) group incidents as problems; 2) focus on substantive problems; 3) push for effective solutions; 4) work systematically to study problems; 5) disaggregate and successfully label problems; 6) analyze the multiple interests inherent in any incident; 7) capture and critique current responses to problems; 8) search uninhibitedly for solutions; 9) adopt a proactive stance; 10) strengthen decision making and accountability; and 11) evaluate their efforts (Goldstein 1990). Under such circumstances, the argument goes, problem-solving police can achieve goals of crime reduction, fear reduction, and public service. Indeed, Guyot (1991) has shown that, when police agencies focus their attention on specific problems and attack those problems aggressively, problem-oriented policing can be very successful.

In many ways, problem-oriented policing can be seen as evolving into the newer notion of "community policing." Consisting more of a set of techniques and attitudes than a coherent theory of police action, community-policing models aim at achieving several goals. In general, community policing is aimed at building a partnership between the police and the community; fostering a problem-solving rather than incident-reacting stance; empowering local residents; increasing accountability for police actions; and providing services for citizens as they need and want them (Austin 1992). Police become, in essence, agents for change who mobilize social resources to empower people, provide services, and work to resolve the problems a community cares about.

The problem-solving orientation is also prevalent in the literature on social work and the social services. Brieland (1995) states, for example, that in the social work field:

> Six steps that are applicable to all methods, approaches, and fields may be distilled from the vast literature: 1) the establishment of contact, 2) the assessment and identification of problems, 3) the identification of goals and service plans, 4) the provision of services, 5) the evaluation of outcomes through group and single-system techniques, [and] 6) feedback and the application of results to future practice (2256).

In other words, social workers are to identify the problems inherent in a given circumstance, establish plans of action to overcome these challenges, and then take action to achieve desired goals within this context.

Decision theory is a powerful tool for understanding how social-service workers, police officers, and other street-level workers make, or ought to make, choices. It offers normative models or ideals for making decisions that are more rational on one hand, and more community-oriented on the other. Additionally, it is proactive and optimistic, suggesting that the worker can successfully overcome problems that are very significant and challenging.

In a case like the one with the baby with a broken leg, the problem-solving approach would require the worker, most likely as part of a team, to first assess the root causes of the situation within both the family and the larger community. This might include consideration of anger management, family therapy, vocational training, career counseling, day care services, housing assistance, legal services, medical care, parenting classes, support networks, substance abuse counseling, and a variety of other issues. The worker would then catalog and assess existing strategies and/or develop new approaches for addressing these problems. Based on this assessment, the worker would then design and implement an action plan. Finally, the worker would evaluate the outcomes and use this information to manage and to prevent such problems in the future.

Although such approaches have some appeal, problem-solving models are subject to a number of important questions when applied to real-world environments. First, the problem-solver role, taken literally, involves an extensive use of public resources. As a practical matter, however, there are far more problems that might be addressed than there are workers, dollars, or hours in the day. It is a resource-intensive approach to public service at a time when public resources are highly constrained.

Second, it is fair to ask whether police can solve seemingly intractable problems like drug dealing or whether social-service workers can solve problems like child abuse. These problems have defied decades of intense political and social action. The problem-solving model may work in specific circumstances, but it seems problematic as a model of daily public-service work.

Further, the public servant as problem solver is essentially a proactive model of public service. The application of intensive solutions to problems presupposes extensive research, program development, and tailor-made services. It also presumes that subjects of this problem solving will respond as expected and change their behavior. Consequently, problem-solver models provide no standards by which worker actions can be described or evaluated when they are responding to unanticipated situations. The truth is, much of public service is reactive—responding to police calls, investigating complaints, providing counseling and support to clients, and so on. Thus, proactive models are of only limited utility in helping workers respond to the incidents they face.

Next, problem-solving models often assume, at their core, that workers and the agencies they represent ought to impose their view of problems and solutions on the community. In other words, the community (or client) is assumed to be sufficiently dysfunctional that an outside actor must intervene to fix things. While this may be the case, it may also not be the case. At one level, problem-solving models are an invitation to send solutions chasing problems, regardless of the apparent legitimacy of those solutions in the eyes of their prospective clients—who, as was discussed previously, are the source of one of the pressures on street-level public servants to exercise discretion in the first place.

Finally, the model places a tremendous burden on workers to define extraordinarily complex social problems and to work with other agencies and the community to design solutions, generate resources, and advocate for community action. At the same time, workers are expected to continue with their regular duties and a typically ever-expanding workload. While such workers can be proactive in defining and attempting to solve problems, they must also be reactive in responding to immediate short-term situations that demand resolution without the time or resources necessary for the linear, analytical problem-solving approach suggested by these theorists.

Cumulatively, then, problem-solving models are useful to the degree that they are optimistic about what workers can achieve, and to the degree that they accurately describe what can occur under the narrow, resource-intensive conditions of their adoption. As broader models of worker action, however, they do not account for the issues of discretion and legitimacy as they arise in contemporary street-level public service.

Model 6: The Political Actor

Finally, some have suggested that bureaucrats be viewed as legitimate and unabashedly political actors. Particularly in the last twenty years, public administration has increasingly acknowledged that it is "part of the governing process, of deciding what is to be done and who shall carry the burden" (McCurdy 1986, 8). Goodsell, for example, suggested that a key issue in the field relates to the development of a new role for public administration as a "teacher of governance" (1990, 503). He argued that "public administration possesses a capacity to instruct society with respect to both the substantive knowledge and normative ideals of governance" (1990, 504). Likewise, the authors of the lead chapter of *Refounding Public Administration* stated:

> Public Administration needs to assert . . . the value and legitimacy of the Public Administrator as an actor in the governing process, and the distinctiveness and worth of his or her role—competence directed to the maintenance of . . . the broadest possible understanding of public interest, and the constitutional governance process (Wamsley et al. 1990, 43).

Similarly, Spicer and Terry (1993) have suggested that administrative discretion is helpful in limiting the discretion of political leaders. This sort of role for public servants has also been expressed as being a matter of organizational citizenship (Golembiewski 1989). From this perspective, public employees retain the rights and responsibilities of citizenship in participating with clients in formulating and implementing public policy. Similarly, proponents of the so-called "new public administration" argue that public administrators must consciously embody social equity and other "democratic" and "constitutional" values. The need for public administration to defend and uphold these values, according to a leading protagonist of new public administration, arises from the fact that "pluralistic government systematically discriminates in favor of established stable bureaucracies . . . and against those minorities . . . who lack political and economic resources" (Frederickson 1971, 426). This is arguably a worthy, but unabashedly political, agenda.

Political action is also advocated in some of the social work literature. The argument is that social services not only seek to change the behavior and address the problems of individuals, but must also attend to changing the environment which produces such problems (Neugeboren 1996). Or, as Hopps and Collins put it, social-service workers should "empower those in acute need and to encourage those in the dominant segment of society that controls the resources and power to meet those needs" (1995, 2271).

Again applied to the case that begins this chapter, political models of street-level public service suggest that in addition to assessing the risks to the child, the capacities of the parents, and so on, the worker *also* ought to have considered how she might need to take action within a larger political and community context.

Was this a matter of social inequity? Had the parents been unfairly disadvantaged and/or were there larger community and political causes for what had occurred? Had they been systematically denied access to the kinds of resources, training, education, and the like that might improve their situation? Could those barriers be removed? As a citizen and community member, what might she do to change the system that created the problem?

As was the case with models of problem solving, the problem with political models is accountability. Such models usefully point to the expanding role of bureaucratic actors in the policy process, but in so doing, fail to: 1) explain how their efforts to defend democratic and constitutional values meld with the efforts of elected officials to do so, and 2) provide standards against which the decisions of workers can be evaluated. While such workers are citizens, they are not elected, and the general public has no direct control over their activities. Moreover, this view of public service offers no insights as to how workers are supposed to decide between competing values. As a consequence, political models do not fully answer the problem of how to exercise street-level discretion effectively and responsibly, and of establishing the legitimacy of worker choices.

DISCRETION, LEGITIMACY, AND EXISTING MODELS OF STREET-LEVEL PUBLIC SERVICE: AN ASSESSMENT

In general, then, existing models of discretionary action share several strengths, yet they suffer from a number of weaknesses. On the positive side of the ledger, bureaucratic models realistically portray the expectations that public employees function in hierarchical structures and that they be impartial and efficient. Public-policy models effectively highlight the necessity and importance of street-level decision making and discretion. Approaches that emphasize professionalism illustrate the influence of professional norms and socialization on organizational behavior. Problem-solving models and models based on the concept of power highlight important facets of frontline public service. Finally, political models challenge the field to find new ways to account for the growing responsibilities and challenges of public service in the context of community demands, intractable societal problems, and vague legislative dictates.

On the negative side, however, these models fail to provide a workable framework for understanding and evaluating street-level bureaucratic discretion in the context of organizational, political, and societal values. They suggest either that worker discretion is inevitable and should just be accepted, that discretion should be controlled without demonstrating how that is to be accomplished, or that bureaucratic discretion in the policy process is to be valued and rewarded without attention to organizational, democratic, and political controls. As such, they offer little guidance to workers, their supervisors, and others about how street-level discretion can be used legitimately and effectively to accomplish public purposes in any particular situation.

What is needed is a model of public service that can embody the strengths of the dominant theories while addressing and answering their weaknesses. Discretion is a central dimension of frontline public service, and the legitimacy of worker decisions must be meaningfully evaluated. In order to address these issues, a new model of public service—street-level leadership—is presented and analyzed in the next chapter.

3

A Model of
Street-Level Leadership

The Work of Street-Level Public Servants:
The Case of the (Really) Dirty Home

A social-service worker was assigned a case that was new to her but was not new to the department: a report of a dirty home that many other workers had visited previously. The children living at the home, the report alleged, came to school with such a foul, sooty odor that they were receiving baths after they arrived. Their clothes were also laden with wood ash. Additionally, one of the children was reported to have had soot in her nostrils every day for over two weeks. The report suggested that there was environmental neglect of the children as well as risk of harm to their well-being.

When she and the observer arrived at the home, the worker began investigating the allegations in the report. The home was, in fact, filled by a smoky odor, as the parents heated it with a wood stove and a fireplace. Substantial amounts of blue smoke—much of it from pressure-treated lumber—was observed billowing out of the fireplace into the living room. The living room temperature, with the fireplace in use, was 46 degrees. The bedrooms, which were in a closed-off part of the home that was not heated during the day, were much colder.

Further, the bedrooms had no finished walls; nails and other obstructions were exposed. Additionally, the entryway between the two rooms the children used as bedrooms was almost entirely blocked by a large kerosene heater pushed up against a bare stud wall. There were no windows in the children's bedrooms; thus, the kerosene heater blocked the only means of exit the children had from their rooms in case of emergency. Electrical wires and sockets were also exposed. Carbon monoxide detectors that the department had recently purchased for the family had gone off once and not been properly reset.

Finally, the home itself was filthy. A one-gallon milk container was open and sitting on a table. Dishes were unwashed; food had remained in the pots in which it was prepared, apparently for some time; and clothes, paper, and other items were scattered on the floor. Further, while there was some food in the home, there was also a substantial quantity of beer.

Having conducted her preliminary investigation of the home, the worker then interviewed the parents. She explained the purpose of her visit—to investigate the environmental neglect report—and discussed her concerns about the exposed wires, billowing smoke, poor temperature, and other conditions in the house. She also discussed their use of alcohol with the parents. Additionally, because the mother had a large wound on her forehead, the worker asked her if she was being physically abused.

The answers the parents gave to the worker's questions were interesting. Both parents said they knew that the children went to school smelling of soot on occasion; however, they claimed they had recently had their water turned back on, and while they did not have the money to pay to have the water heated, they did give the children nightly sponge baths. Clothes were washed at a laundry on an intermittent basis. Neither parent worked, and they admitted that they had not paid their heating bills in some time and that was why they were forced to heat with wood. They also claimed to be repairing the exposed walls and taking care to provide power only to the wires in use at a given moment by turning the fuses to each circuit on and off. (When asked to demonstrate this, the father turned on an appliance plugged into a supposedly "off" circuit; the device came on instantly.) As for alcohol use, the mother stated she had been in a treatment facility for alcohol abuse but had not completed the program;

the man indicated that he consumed only small amounts of alcohol and then only on the weekends. Both parents stated that they thought their use of alcohol was "fine." Finally, on the question of domestic violence, the woman said she "falls down," particularly when intoxicated, and had hurt herself in one such fall.

In addition to answering the worker's questions, the parents also complained that they were being harassed. The man insisted that "a poor man can't get a break," and both parents insisted that there was a neighbor who was trying to get them into trouble by reporting them to the department. In response, the worker explained the law regarding the use of department workers to perpetrate harassment and suggested that the parents could take steps to act on their allegations. She then left the residence.

After leaving the home, the worker indicated a strong desire to remove the children from the home and place them in protective custody. The living conditions, the likelihood of parental alcohol abuse, and the indications of domestic violence all suggested, she said, that the children were at a substantial risk of harm. Thus she wanted to place the children in long-term protective custody.

Importantly, while the worker admitted that she had the authority under the law to remove the children from the home, this authority was only temporary. Local prosecutors would have to participate in any process resulting in longer-term removal of the children from the home. So unless they were convinced that the problems were severe enough to warrant action, the children would likely be returned home to the risks the worker thought were severe. When she called the prosecutor's office to apprise them of her desire, however, they indicated no interest in participating in such a process. They were familiar with the case, having had many reports of apparent abuse or neglect about this family before, and saw no significant differences between this incident and past reports.

Frustrated by the prosecutors' lack of support, the worker made several phone calls in an attempt to gather evidence for her position. She called the local heating company to investi-

gate the status of the family's service and to ask them to check on the carbon monoxide levels in the home. She also called local fire officials to ask them to inspect the home's wiring as a fire hazard.

The reports returned by both the heating and fire officials were very supportive of the worker's position. The heating company employee who visited the home indicated that the carbon monoxide levels in the home when he arrived were well above safety limits. Even after opening all the doors and windows for an hour and airing the home out the carbon monoxide level was only barely acceptable. This employee also noted that the fireplace in the living room was a gas fireplace that was being improperly and dangerously used to burn wood. Local fire officials did not even enter the home before declaring that it was a substantial fire risk; the flue being used to vent the living room fireplace was determined to be undersized from an exterior inspection. (It also later turned out to be made of conventional heating flue aluminum.)

Armed with this additional information, the worker again called local prosecutors. This time, they agreed to support a process to take longer-term custody of the children and authorized the worker to remove the children from the home. She then called local police, entered the home, assisted the children in gathering their clothes and school needs, took them for a medical examination, and turned them over to a local foster parent.

INTRODUCTION

So far, this book has focused on the complex environment of public service, the changing nature and scope of worker discretion, the need to consider the legitimacy of worker choices, and why existing models of public service do not adequately capture these facets of public service. This chapter explores why and how the work of street-level public servants can be seen as leadership and how doing so provides a framework for both understanding worker discretion and making judgments about the legitimacy of their choices.

WHY LEADERSHIP?

This book argues that leadership provides a workable theoretical basis for integrating the concepts of discretion, legitimacy, and accountability into a model of street-level public service. Unfortunately, no phenomenon of social life is more discussed, more controversial, and less understood than the concept of leadership. There is not even one commonly accepted definition of what leadership is. For example, leadership has been variously described as "the process of persuasion or example by which an individual . . . induces a group to pursue objectives held by the leader or shared by the leader and his or her followers" (Gardner 1990, 1), "exercised when persons with certain motives and purposes mobilize, in competition or conflict with others, institutional, political, psychological, and other resources so as to arouse, engage, and satisfy the motives of followers" (Burns 1978, 18), and "the process of influencing the activities of an individual or group in efforts toward goal achievement in a given situation" (Hersey, Blanchard, and Johnson 1996, 91). Stogdill, in fact, concluded that "there are as many definitions of leadership as there are persons who have attempted to define the concept" (Stogdill 1974, 259).

Not only are there definitional problems, there also seems to be a kind of awestruck skepticism of leaders and the concept of leadership in both the academic literature and popular culture. Leaders can inspire; they can also subvert. Leaders can build; they can also destroy. Leaders can achieve; they can also corrupt. If this is so, of what value is the notion of leadership? Is leadership the simple exercise of power, or is it something more? Do leaders require an ethical base for action? Questions of who leaders are, what they do, and how they do it are inevitably as controversial as they are significant.

Despite these problems, controversies, and limitations, we argue that leadership provides a useful and compelling framework for understanding the challenges of frontline public service. The reasons for the appeal of the leadership model can be briefly summarized as follows.

First, leadership can be seen to encompass a variety of behaviors. Leaders, for example, may exercise unilateral authority and power in order to achieve a goal in some circumstances. Alternatively, they may act to inspire and empower individuals or groups to articulate and achieve goals themselves. Because public servants are expected to employ numerous approaches to accomplishing public objectives, this capacity to accommodate a wide range of behaviors and strategies is important.

Second, the concept of leadership demands a consideration of values. In this sense, it is the missing link in existing models—by focusing on values it provides the bridge between the leader's use of power and the legitimacy of those actions, between the norms of professionalism and the context of democratic governance. As Denhardt (1984) states, ". . . Public administration is concerned with managing change processes in pursuit of publicly defined societal values" (17). The notion of leadership provides a means to consider these values in the context of bureaucracy, accountability, and governance. As such, it can be used to build on the strengths of existing models and to address their primary weaknesses—the failure to address the issue of accountability and the role of values in understanding administrative discretion in the governance process.

Third, leadership models provide concepts and standards by which the appropriateness and legitimacy of specific actions can be evaluated. Street-level leaders can be more or less effective in achieving the goals that the society, community, organization, and law may expect them to achieve. Both the effectiveness and the legitimacy of their actions can be evaluated in reference to standards embodied in leadership theory.

Fourth, the language of leadership offers a positive and powerful way to talk about the role of street-level public servants and, at the same time, convey the need to consider this role in a larger context. Leaders do not operate in a vacuum—leaders are accountable to both their superiors and their followers within a larger context of values, norms, and expectations. This is the position of street-level leaders in public service. These public employees work in environments that are often highly conflictual and in which they must negotiate and balance sometimes-competing demands and values of the community, politicians, organizational rules, personal and professional values, and the dictates of the situation at hand. Moreover, because of the nature of their work, they sometimes must make their choices largely independently. To portray the challenges and demands these workers face as being simply a matter of morality, ethics, institutional and regime values, bureaucratic responsibility, professionalism, or good judgment is incomplete. It is all of those things simultaneously. While this may make street-level public service appear to be an "impossible job" (Hargrove and Glidewell 1990), it may nonetheless be understood as demanding a special form of leadership.

Fifth, leadership theory is a useful framework for understanding the jobs of street-level public servants because it speaks to the two types of discretion they are called upon to exercise: discretion over means (or process) and discretion over ends (or outcomes). Public servants, under differing circumstances, may exercise discretion in deciding both what to do *and* how to do it. Accordingly, they may need to act as different types of leaders in different contexts. For these and other reasons explored more fully in the pages that follow, we argue that the concept of leadership offers a promising and important alternative lens for viewing the work of street-level public servants.

LEADERSHIP AND POWER IN THE CONTEXT OF STREET-LEVEL PUBLIC SERVICE

In a general sense, then, there are a number of reasons why leadership can be argued to be a useful way to look at the challenges of frontline public service. The application of specific models of leadership to street-level public service is complicated, however, because there are a number of different perspectives that can be considered. Some of these perspectives are more useful than others in terms of their application to the work of street-level public servants.

Although there is considerable variation, much of the literature on leadership can be grouped around four basic perspectives or types of models: trait, behavioral, situational, and transformational. In this section, each of these alternative conceptions of leadership and the use of power in the practice of leadership is considered in terms of its usefulness as a lens for viewing the issues of discretion and legitimacy in the work of street-level public servants.

Trait Theories of Leadership

Probably the oldest approach to the study of leadership is trait theory. Put simply, trait theory holds that leadership is based on inborn, innate characteristics that are predominantly psychological in nature (Carlyle 1840; Galton 1869; Argyris 1955; Sank 1974;

Stogdill 1974). In this view of leadership, individual traits such as originality, popularity, self-confidence, sociability, judgment, aggressiveness, humor, desire to excel, adaptability, assertiveness, decisiveness, and cooperativeness, among others, combine to inspire others and cause them to follow the leader's agenda (Bass 1990; Stogdill 1974; Kirkpatrick and Locke 1991; Nahavandi 1997). According to trait theory, then, leaders are born rather than made.

There is some research that suggests that certain traits increase the likelihood of leadership effectiveness (Yukl 1994). Bennis (1984), for example, found that leaders tend to share four common traits or areas of competence: management of attention, management of meaning, management of trust, and management of self. Mills and Bohannon (1980) found that police officers who possessed the traits of dominance, intelligence, and autonomy were more effective than those who did not. Additionally, Kirkpatrick and Locke (1991) demonstrated that the dominant traits associated with leadership are important in that they encourage individuals to acquire the skills, resources, and power they need to achieve their goals. Conversely, some traits have been suggested as disqualifying an individual for leadership: not understanding issues that are important to followers, being nonparticipative, and being rigid (Geier 1967).

While there can be no doubt that personality traits affect the practice of leadership just as they affect every other dimension of human life, such studies hold only limited utility for understanding street-level public service. The main value of trait approaches is that they highlight the importance of the personal characteristics the worker brings to the job. But, as depicted in Figure 1 in Chapter One, worker characteristics are only one of a matrix of factors which influence workers in street-level public service. Thus, trait theories present only an incomplete picture of public-service leadership on the street.

There are other problems with the application of trait theory to street-level public service as well. First, such studies tend to focus on the political, social, and business elite. While this is true to an extent with all types of leadership studies, the heavy reliance of trait theory on the characteristics of leaders at the "top" makes it less than ideal in terms of its applicability to public servants who work at the "bottom" of their organizations.

Second, trait studies tend not to take the circumstances in which the leader operates into consideration. Leadership behavior is considered to be a relatively fixed manifestation of the underlying traits of the leader. This view of leadership, then, does not account for the variability that was often observed in the work of street-level public servants. It also does not meaningfully account for the variety of situational factors described in Figure 1 that can be seen to shape worker choices.

Third, trait approaches, at best, only finesse the problem of legitimacy. That is, it is as possible for a decisive, sociable, assertive leader to use his or her traits to accomplish ends that are corrupt as it is to use them for more worthy goals. In order to overcome this problem, the concept of democratic leadership, or integrity, or some other legitimating concept has to be introduced as a means to ensure that a leader's influence is not used for self-serving or socially unacceptable purposes. This is a "trust me" approach that is, at best, incomplete and awkward, particularly in the case of public servants who are answerable to a variety of legal, organizational, and democratic constraints. As was discussed in the last chapter, something more than "trust me" needs to be offered up as a way of accounting for the legitimacy of leader actions.

Fourth, trait theory is a largely closed view in terms of who can and cannot be a leader. Since one is effectively born with the "correct" leadership traits, there is little that can be done once an individual has been hired. If workers do not possess these traits, there is little hope for them to acquire them. Moreover, as applied to public service, this approach suggests that if an organization wants street-level leaders, it should hire individuals with particular traits and then simply turn them loose to lead.

Trait theories also tend to subsume questions of resources, skills, techniques, and so on, under the power of the individual leader's personality. While such variables may emerge in case studies, they are not given much attention within the context of the model. This, at best, paints an incomplete picture of the realities of leadership.

Finally, there is little in trait theory that lets analysts, citizens, or other interested parties distinguish between individuals who are practicing leadership and those who are merely exercising power. The expression of certain traits, such as charisma, decisiveness, aggressiveness, etc., might be seen as expressions of power rather than acts of leadership. Accordingly, trait theories seem inadequate for fully explaining what leadership *is* and how it can be distinguished from power.

Cumulatively, the strengths and weaknesses of trait theories of leadership suggest that while personality characteristics may help to explain variations in the successes and failures of individual leaders, they do not adequately account for the complexities of either the context of leadership or the standards by which it might be legitimated. As such, they usefully highlight the role of the individual in specific contexts, but do not fully establish those individuals in the complex system of organizations, laws, norms, and communities in which they operate. This is particularly problematic as it relates to street-level public servants since, as Figure 1 in Chapter One suggests, the environment of street-level public service is complex and multifaceted. Trait theories, then, do not fully apply to leadership as practiced "on the street."

Leadership as Behavior

Partly as a response to criticisms of trait theory, a later generation of scholars focused on leadership as a set of behaviors rather than traits. These scholars argued that it was less important to possess a particular set of personal characteristics than it was to engage in leadership behaviors that would achieve desired results from followers. Some of these behavioral approaches emphasized the importance of employee-centered and participative forms of leadership (Lewin, Lippitt, and White 1939; Likert 1961; Argyris 1964). In these models, it was suggested that leadership behavior which demonstrated a concern for employees and the use of participative techniques for decision making would result in improved performance.

Other behavioral models of leadership promoted the idea that leaders ought to engage in behaviors that were both employee-oriented *and* directive (Blake and Mouton 1964). Much of this work grew out of two important research programs in the 1940s and 1950s at the Ohio State University and the University of Michigan. In the Ohio State studies, researchers used questionnaires designed to provide information on the observed behavior of leaders in a wide variety of organizations. They found that leadership behavior fell into two main categories, *initiating structure* (the extent to which the leader structures his or her role and the role of subordinates in accomplishing a task) and *consideration* (the extent to which a leader shows concern for subordinates and behaves in a supportive manner). The Michigan leadership studies used a similar, two-dimensional approach to leadership, but called the categories "employee orientation" and "production orientation." Michigan researchers found that effective leaders engaged in both task-oriented and relationship-oriented behavior (Likert 1967).

Some research suggests that the behavioral approach to understanding leadership can have some explanatory power in describing leadership successes and failures. It has been shown, for example, that leaders who consider the needs and desires of their followers and provide support for subordinates tend to build worker satisfaction, loyalty, and trust—each of which can be expected to enhance performance and goal achievement (Likert 1961; Atwater 1988; Seltzer and Numerof 1988). Clarifying objectives and structuring workers' environments in ways that support the leader's agenda have also been shown to influence leadership effectiveness (House, Filley, and Gujarati 1971). Other research has found that both directiveness and supportiveness are important (Greene and Schriesheim 1980).

Viewed from the perspective of street-level public servants, behavioral leadership theory has some advantages over trait theory. First, behavioral theory is inherently more open in terms of who can be a leader. Since behaviors can be learned, it is possible to train workers to behave as leaders, and thus develop a cadre of leader–workers who can inspire and direct groups and communities toward desired goals. Unlike trait theory, then, individuals are not prisoners of their personalities.

Additionally, behavioral theory's explicit focus on skills, resources, tools, and techniques takes the *process* of leadership more seriously than does trait theory. Leaders, after all, have to act; they have to *do* things in order to achieve their goals. Behavioral theories of leadership more completely account for the things that leaders *do* (as opposed to what leaders *are*) than does trait theory.

Finally, behavioral theories do a somewhat better job of explaining leadership effectiveness than do trait theories. By focusing on the behaviors and actions of leaders as they work to influence their followers, behavioral theories of leadership provide a more comprehensive account of leadership in action. Consequently, behavioral theories provide a more realistic and action-oriented framework within which the work of street-level public servants might be understood.

While behavioral models have a number of strengths in terms of their applicability to street-level public service, they also have some significant weaknesses. Such theories do not, for example, do a very good job of taking contextual factors into account. That is, by focusing on behaviors, such theories assume that by using the correct leadership behavior (which combines attention to both the task at hand and the human element) success is likely. But it is possible that even if a leader does all the right things, employs all the right behaviors, the leader will still fail. Put in the context of Figure 1, then, behaviors may not fully explain either what leadership is or why it succeeds and fails in different contexts.

Second, such theories have, at best, an incomplete accounting for the legitimacy of leader behaviors. The primary standard implied in behavioral models of leadership is whether the leader's behavior reflected both a task orientation and a people orientation. In public service, where workers are answerable to broader and often-conflicting values, simply behaving as leaders according to these models may not be enough to legitimate their actions. Structuring tasks and giving people support is laudable, but if the goal is corrupt, such leadership behaviors can be argued to be illegitimate. Street-level public servants work in a context that requires the legitimacy of their actions to be established, not simply assumed.

Along related grounds, it is not always clear in behavioral theories why the actions being described are exercises in leadership rather than power. The "power of persuasion" is well known (Neustadt 1986); thus, what distinguishes the behaviors such theories describe as "leadership" is not inherently obvious. Some attention to the differences between leadership and power wielding is required before leadership behaviors can be fully understood.

Taken together, behavioral theories of leadership usefully relate to frontline public service to the degree that they recognize that leadership is made up of acts or behaviors. Moreover, behavioral models usefully separate the act of leadership from the personalities of those who exercise it. They do not, however, provide ready standards for legitimating particular leadership actions or goals. They also do not adequately distinguish leadership from power or account for the complex variables that may shape a leader's effectiveness in a particular context.

Situational Approaches to Leadership

A third way to look at leadership is to focus on the relationship between the situation or context in which leadership is taking place and the actions, goals, attitudes, and behaviors of specific leaders. Situational theories argue, at their core, that effective leadership is based on the relationship between leaders and followers in a particular context, and that a specific leader's effectiveness can best be explained by examining the "match" between the leader's style, decisions, and behaviors and the circumstances in which the leader is acting (Fiedler 1970; Hersey and Blanchard 1988; House 1971; House and Mitchell 1974; Stinson and Johnson 1975; Fiedler and Chemers 1982; Vroom and Yetton 1973; Vroom and Jago 1988). Thus, issues like the cooperativeness of followers, the resources with which the leader can act, the nature of the task, the ability of followers, and other situational factors are crucial determinants of the effectiveness of leadership.

Different models focus on different situational factors as being the most important in determining the most effective leadership style. In Fiedler's Contingency Theory of Leadership, for example, three major situational variables dictate whether leaders should engage in behavior that is primarily task-oriented or relationship-oriented: 1) the personal relationship of the leader with the followers, 2) how highly structured the task is, and 3) the power and authority of the leader's position (Fiedler 1970). The Vroom–Yetton Contingency Model of Leadership, on the other hand, suggests that the situational factors a leader should consider in choosing a leadership style include the importance of the quality of the decision, the availability of information, the extent to which the problem is structured, the importance of subordinate acceptance of a decision, subordinates' commitment to organizational goals, and the expected level of conflict (Vroom and Yetton 1973).

One of the best-known models of situational leadership is the Hersey and Blanchard (1988) Tri-Dimensional Leadership Effectiveness Model. In this model, it is the follower's readiness to achieve the leader's goal(s) that shapes the leader's actions. According to Hersey and Blanchard (1988), in situations where the follower is unwilling and unable to act, the leader must be directive and "tell" the follower what to do by providing specific instructions and closely supervising performance. In circumstances where the follower remains unable but becomes more compliant or willing, leaders should "sell" or explain the task and provide opportunity for clarification. When followers are able to act but lack willingness or confidence to act, the model prescribes that leaders must participate with followers by sharing ideas and facilitating decision making. Finally, when followers are both able and willing to act, leaders should "delegate" by allowing followers to take responsibility and carry out tasks.

In looking at situational leadership models, it is important to distinguish between leadership actions that are *successful* in producing the desired response and leadership behaviors that are what Bass (1960) terms *effective*. Success simply has to do with whether the leader's action results in a desired change in the behavior of others. A leader, for example, may consistently use highly coercive techniques, no matter what the situation is. These coercive techniques may be relatively successful most of the time in terms of getting people to do what the leader wants. This is not the same, however, as leadership effectiveness in Bass's view. Leadership effectiveness speaks not only to whether the leader succeeds in accomplishing the desired objective, but also to how a leader's approach affects the follower. As such, while success only considers the needs of the leader, effectiveness considers the needs of both the leader and follower. As Bass (1960) points out, effective leadership makes people more likely to follow such leaders in the future.

As a consequence of the distinction between successful and effective leadership, an important assumption in situational leadership models is that the leader should provide only what is "missing" in a particular circumstance. In other words, if the situation needs structure, the leader should provide structure. Conversely, if the situation involves followers who need encouragement, leaders should undertake to provide it. In the Hersey and Blanchard (1988) model, for example, the most effective leadership behavior is to provide only that level of directiveness and support needed to achieve task accomplishment. Additionally, leadership effectiveness, rather than being an either/or proposition, is represented by a continuum ranging from very effective to very ineffective, depending on the degree of congruence between leadership style and the situation.

Taken together, then, situational theories of leadership focus on developing and implementing the most effective strategies by which leaders can achieve particular goals in specific contexts. If a leader correctly assesses situational variables and chooses strategies that are appropriate to those circumstances, the leader can be effective. Effective leaders, then, integrate contextual factors into their choice making.

As was the case with the other theories of leadership addressed earlier in this chapter, there is some evidence that situational models can be useful in explaining leadership effectiveness. Those leaders who recognize situational variables, determine what resources and constraints they face, and then match their leadership style and behaviors to these realities have been shown to be more effective at achieving their goals than those who do not make such a determination (Ayman, Chemers, and Fiedler 1995; Peters, Hartke, and Pohlmann 1985; Crouch and Yetton 1987; Jago and Vroom 1980). As such, circumstances matter in the effective exercise of leadership.

Clearly, models of situational leadership have much to say in regard to the work that street-level public servants do. As shown in Figure 1 in Chapter One, there are a number of situational factors that can shape the environment in which a worker makes decisions. The presence or absence of the media, the relative cooperativeness and support of clients, crowds, and supervisors, as well as the applicability of department rules, may all shape the kinds of decisions workers make and the range of actions they take. Accordingly, situational leadership models can be expected to be very useful in understanding and evaluating the work that street-level public servants do.

Because they emphasize leadership effectiveness, rather than simply success, situational leadership models also provide a useful framework for assessing the legitimacy of the *means* employed by leaders to accomplish their objectives. As applied to street-level leadership, if a worker unnecessarily uses coercive power with a citizen, that citizen is likely to be left worse off in terms of his or her likely attitude and behavior toward dealing with police officers, social-service workers, or other frontline workers in the future. The citizen may comply, but is not likely to cooperate or change his or her behavior for the better. Moreover, other citizens, bystanders, the media, coworkers, and others may also be negatively affected if a worker's behavior is inconsistent with the needs of the situation. So within the situational leadership framework, assessing the legitimacy of workers' choices about how they will accomplish their goals involves consideration of both immediate success and the effectiveness of their actions in a broader sense.

For street-level public servants, then, situational models are useful in helping workers to recognize the importance of situational variables in matching style and behaviors to circumstances in order to choose successful, effective, and therefore legitimate means to reach their goals. Again, however, as was the case with the other theories of leadership described earlier, there are also limitations to situational models. While these models provide useful guidance in determining what sorts of leadership behaviors can be expected to be more or less effective in a given situation, they are largely silent on the question of the "ends" of leadership. In other words, these models do not speak to the question of whether the goals or objectives being sought are legitimate, only to the best way to accomplish them. When the goals to be achieved are "given," such as when a police officer is required by law to take a suspect into custody, the use of power can be judged to be more or less legitimate, based on the premises of situational leadership models. This is not always the case, however. Sometimes the legitimacy of the goals themselves is open to question. Accordingly, situational leadership theories present only a partial model of the types of decisions street-level public servants are called upon to make and the legitimacy of the power they exercise.

Power and the Practice of Leadership

As already explained, trait, behavioral, and situational models of leadership do not fully address the use of power because they do not speak to the legitimacy of the ends being sought through its use. To be legitimate, power must be used to accomplish purposes which are themselves legitimate. As Russell (1938) argued, power as an end is inherently undesirable, but power as a means can be desirable. Accordingly, the concept of power needs to be more closely examined so that its role in the exercise of legitimate street-level discretion can be understood.

So what is power and how can its use be evaluated? Typically, power has been defined as Robert Dahl does: "A has power over B to the extent that he can get B to do something that B would not otherwise do" (Dahl 1957, 202–203). In this "first face" of power (Lukes 1974), power is a direct exchange between actors in which one of the actors exerts more control over the outcome than the other. Individuals with more power, whatever its sources, can be expected to be relatively more successful in achieving their goals than those with less power.

But the use of power is often more complicated than that. Even recognizing the use of power can be difficult, in part because power is the *potential* to control or influence another. As Ott put it, power is "the latent ability to influence others' actions, thoughts, or emotions" (1989, 420). Once expressed, power becomes something else—authority or force (Bierstedt 1950), or sometimes an act of leadership.

So the exercise of power can take many forms. For example, it is not always in the interest of those with power to engage in an open struggle. When individuals engage in a power struggle, one side typically loses. From the perspective of those with established positions, a visible loss erodes their latent power or their ability to prevail in future struggles. So, logically, it makes sense for those with relatively established power to work to systematically avoid or exclude challenges. These exclusionary actions have been termed power's "second face" (Lukes 1974).

There is also a "third face" of power. In this third face, the power wielder convinces others that what they really want is what the power wielder wants. As Lukes puts it, "A may exercise power over B by getting him to do what he does not want to do, but he also exercises power over him by influencing, shaping, or determining his very wants. . . . This may happen in the absence of observable conflict, which may have been successfully averted" (1974, 23). The successful use of power's third face, then, might insulate the powerful from challenge simply because the powerful are able to convince potential challengers that there is no reason to challenge them in the first place.

Because power can take so many forms, and because its use by frontline workers can so profoundly influence the street-level realities of law, justice, and governance, it is important to focus on the legitimacy of its use in that context. Particularly in the public sector, Friedrich argues that the authoritative exercise of power *must* be based on legitimacy and grounded in reason and values. He states, ". . . Power thus reinforced by authority acquires the capacity to create law that is right and just by making it legitimate" (1963, 204). Clearly, street-level workers, just like other public leaders, exercise power. Police officers and social workers, for example, can exercise "first face" power in arresting people or removing children from homes. They can also exercise "second face" power by deciding whether or not to work with clients or by avoiding situations where they are likely to lose, such as in a potential riot situation. To the degree that their actions shape clients' self-perceptions, attitudes, and values, they can exercise "third face" power as well, such as when a social worker convinces parents to change how they view the process of being investigated for child abuse or neglect, from a situation of threat to one of opportunity for assistance.

The use of all of these faces of power can be either legitimate or illegitimate. For example, one of the social-service workers observed for this book had been working with a father and son for a number of months, and although she was very concerned about the boy's well-being, for a number of reasons she had not been able to develop a defensible case for his removal from the home. The father was mentally disturbed and possibly brain damaged from a near-fatal motorcycle accident several years before. He was convinced that both God and his ex-wife spoke to him through the metal plate in his head and that his house was controlled by the devil. He refused mental health treatment and drugs. His home was occupied by a changing group of drug addicts and street people. While he was in and out of jail for writing bad checks, shoplifting, and petty theft, his eight-year-old son would be cared for by whoever was in the home. Despite these circumstances, the man and his son were very close and affectionate when they were together. Although there had been several reports on the boy, particularly when the father was in jail, the father had always been able to patch together a minimally adequate arrangement for his son. On this day, the man had been in jail for almost a week and the school nurse had called to complain that the boy had arrived dirty, hungry, and in need of medical care.

One of the authors accompanied the worker as she went to the home to check on the situation while the boy was at school. When she arrived, she found five people in the living room, some asleep and the others too "high" to respond to her questions. She found a woman and her daughter staying in the back of the house, however, who had cared for the boy previously. The worker knew the woman from past visits and thought that she would, indeed, attempt to care for the boy. Nonetheless, the worker was not convinced that the situation would work in the long term, in part because the woman could not, or would not, do anything about the people in the living room.

Rather than remove the boy and attempt to gain custody through the courts, a process she had little confidence in for this particular case, the worker decided to visit the father in jail in order to convince him to voluntarily sign a custody agreement which would turn his son over to his brother in another state. The worker and observer drove to the jail and spoke with the father. The conversation was at times lucid, at times bizarre. The man explained how his power of love could fix all problems (even those of the worker, he said) and that his dental fillings were beginning to transmit voices. He was able, however, to talk cogently about his son and the need for him to be safe and cared for. In the end, the worker convinced the father that it was in his interests to sign the agreement, because, she told him, it would allow him to straighten himself out, get rid of the "evil" house, and serve his time without worrying about his son. In doing so, she clearly decided not to use the "first face" of power, but rather exercised the "second face" in moving the child out of state, and the "third face" in convincing the father to change how he viewed relinquishing custody of his son.

Thus, workers can exercise multiple types of power in choosing goals in the situations they face. The issue is not whether street-level workers should exercise such power; the nature of their work and the problems they confront require them to do so. The critical question is: Is this power exercised legitimately or not?

Leadership and the Legitimation of Power

So how, then, can the exercise of power be legitimated in street-level public service? James MacGregor Burns, in his seminal text *Leadership* (1978), provides a number of important insights on this issue. Burns argues that power alone, without moral purpose and reasoned values, will not satisfy the need for "compelling and creative leadership" (1978, 1). Like Russell (1938), he categorizes the use of power according to the motives of the individual exercising it. But Burns uses three categories: the power wielder, the ruler, and the leader. Each is characterized by the relationship between the individual exercising power and the needs and wants of followers.

In describing power wielders, for example, Burns quotes Lasswell in arguing that the "power holder may be the person whose 'private motives are displaced onto public objects and rationalized in terms of public interest'" (Burns 1978, 13). Put another way,

The motives of the power wielders may or may not coincide with what the respondent wants done; it is P's [the power wielder's] intention that controls. Power wielders may or may not recognize respondents' wants and needs; if they do, they may recognize them only to the degree necessary to achieve their own goals (Burns 1978, 14–15).

Thus, power wielders are those who use power for their own gain. In doing so, they *may* satisfy their followers' wants and needs, but this is incidental to the power wielder's goals and agendas.

Rulers, in contrast to power wielders, act in accord with what followers understand to be their wants and needs, but the relationship is one-sided in the ruler's favor. Writing of political elites like absolute monarchs and even modern dictators, Burns argues that, "Rulers had the right to command, subjects the obligation to obey. Only a few complained. The fundamental need of the people was for order and security; obedience seemed a fair exchange for survival" (Burns 1978, 24). Thus, in exchange for security and stability, followers allow rulers virtually absolute political power.

According to Burns, *leaders* are distinguished from both power wielders and rulers in two ways: 1) they act in accord with both their own needs and wants *and* those of their followers; and 2) they act "in a condition of *conflict* or *competition* in which leaders contend in appealing to the motive bases of potential followers" (Burns 1978, 18, emphasis in original). Put another way, leaders derive legitimacy for their use of power based on the wants and needs of their followers under conditions where there is conflict or competition between values and goals. This means that leaders are accountable to followers in ways that power wielders and rulers are not. Because of this accountability, the influence process flows in both directions. Leaders clearly influence the behavior and beliefs of followers, but followers just as clearly influence leaders. In this way, the term "followers" can be understood to represent those to whom the leader is responsible, and whose values and wants the leader's objectives and actions must reflect.

The use of power to set goals, then, can be legitimated through its relationship to the ideals, values, wants, and needs of those whom the leader is seeking to influence. Accordingly, the use of power is legitimate only to the degree that it is used toward the broader ends of the organization, group, or community. Goal attainment or "success," in and of itself, is not sufficient to establish the appropriateness of a given leader's actions and decisions, or even to establish that an individual is a leader at all.

Of course, different individuals, organizations, communities, and so on are likely to disagree over what goals and needs are important. As a result, some individuals might argue that an action is illegitimate because it is inconsistent with what they want. Burns is not suggesting that all needs and wants must be satisfied. Instead, he argues that leadership is often practiced under conditions where there is competition and conflict over what goals ought to be pursued. His model suggests that leaders must consider multiple and competing values and needs, and find a way to balance them in a manner that leads to another, higher set of goals and values. He contrasts this form of leadership, which he calls transformational leadership, with transactional leadership in which leaders give followers something they want in exchange for their performance and support.

Transformational leaders focus their efforts and make their choices based on goals, values, and ideals which they discern that the group, organization, or community wants and ought to advance. Transformational leaders help others to articulate goals and then take action to help achieve them. As Burns states, ". . . The transforming leader looks for potential motives in followers, seeks to satisfy higher needs, and engages the full person of the follower" (1978, 4). Judgments about the appropriateness or legitimacy of leadership actions are then grounded in the underlying values, goals, and ideals of followers. When the leader is working to advance shared values and satisfy higher needs, his or her actions can be seen as legitimate. When, however, the leader takes action that is not based on these values, or perhaps runs counter to a community's ideals and goals, the leader's actions may be seen as illegitimate. The exercise of power may be a component of this process, but a leader's use of power is legitimated only by the underlying goals, values, and desires inherent to the group, organization, or community itself (Burns 1978).

Looked at from this perspective, the concept of leadership can be used as the basis of assessing the legitimacy of discretionary choices by workers. As suggested in Chapter Two, street-level workers exercise discretion over process, over outcomes, and sometimes both. In either case, the notion of leadership can serve as a foundation for addressing questions of legitimacy. Using situational leadership models, the legitimacy of worker choices about process can be based on an assessment of the needs inherent in the situation which the worker confronts. Likewise, using transformational leadership models, the legitimacy of worker choices about goals or outcomes can be assessed based on the values, needs, and preferences embodied within the matrix of influences in which the worker operates.

Leadership, then, is a multidimensional concept that embodies power, discretion, and legitimacy. Leadership is a two-way relationship in which the leader exerts influence but is also influenced by and accountable to others. Leaders take actions and influence others toward goals that are grounded in the wants and values of those who are led. Leadership takes place under conditions of competing values and goals, however. To be both effective and legitimate, leaders must find ways to balance competing needs and wants, and to build on shared values.

UNDERSTANDING STREET-LEVEL
PUBLIC SERVANTS AS LEADERS

It might be possible, of course, to agree with the definition of leadership developed here and yet find its applicability to street-level public service improbable. Such workers, as was noted in Chapter One, do not intuitively spring to mind whenever the word "leadership" is spoken. So how, then, can frontline public servants lead?

According to the definition of leadership developed here, the heart of the concept of leadership is the relationship that leaders have with followers. In fact, leadership cannot be understood without reference to followers. As noted in the preceding discussion, however, the term "followers," as it is used here, suggests more than just acceptance or obedience. *Followers are not only those whom the leader seeks to influence, but also those to whom the leader is accountable. It is based on their values, their wants, and their preferences that leadership is established and legitimated.* Viewing followers from this perspective, who are the followers of frontline public servants? In order to answer this question, it is useful to return again to Figure 1.

Simply stated, the answer to the question of who street-level public servants lead is "everyone and everything in Figure 1." In Chapter One, these variables were described in terms of the ways in which they could influence worker decision making. Then, in Chapter Two, the ways that the interplay of these variables required workers to exercise discretion was examined. But just as these factors directly and indirectly influence workers, workers also exert influence in relation to these factors. Citizen expectations influence workers, but worker actions also influence citizen expectations. Laws create the parameters for worker actions, but the manner in which workers apply the law not only influences its actual implementation, but also may influence lawmakers to modify the law. Supervisors influence workers, but workers also influence supervisors. Media coverage may influence workers, but worker actions also influence media coverage. In other words, workers both influence and are influenced by all of the competing norms, values, and preferences of the individuals and organizations represented in Figure 1.

These variables not only influence and are influenced by the worker; they also represent points of accountability for worker actions. As discussed in Chapter One, workers must comply with the law. But in deciding how to do so, they must also consider a myriad of other interests and values to which they are accountable—supervisors, public opinion, court decisions, client needs, and so on. Simply put, workers exert influence in many arenas by exercising discretion. When they do so, they incur an obligation and responsibility to be accountable within those spheres of influence.

By deciding to remove the children from the dirty home, for example, the worker whose story heads this chapter was exercising leadership by committing public resources and seeking to influence others toward a particular goal. That goal reflected a balance of competing norms and preferences and was based on a shared, higher value. Moreover, the worker pursued that goal with a clear recognition of the multiple layers of accountability that had to be considered.

Thus, in making discretionary choices in a potentially conflictual environment, workers are effectively leading others at the same time they are influenced by and accountable to them. The decisions they make have the effect of influencing their clients, their organizations, and their communities. In the process of exerting this influence, workers also acquire a responsibility and accountability to those whom they influence. As such, street-level public servants can be leaders—so long as the actions they take and the decisions they make are legitimated, based on the values, norms, and preferences embodied within their arena of influence.

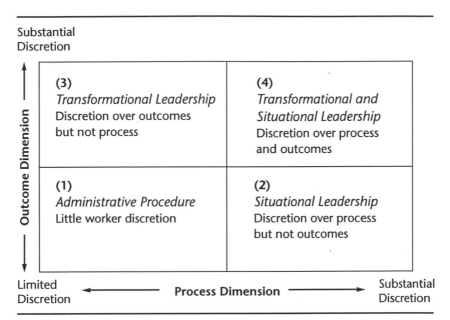

Substantial
Discretion

Outcome Dimension

(3) *Transformational Leadership* Discretion over outcomes but not process	**(4)** *Transformational and Situational Leadership* Discretion over process and outcomes
(1) *Administrative Procedure* Little worker discretion	**(2)** *Situational Leadership* Discretion over process but not outcomes

Limited   ← **Process Dimension** →   Substantial
Discretion   Discretion

Table 1. Dimensions of Street-Level Leadership

A MODEL OF STREET-LEVEL LEADERSHIP

Which leadership models are most useful in understanding how workers can face the challenges of street-level public service? Depending on the circumstances and the kinds of choices workers are called upon to make, different types of leadership are needed. In order to illustrate how different contexts call for different types of leadership approaches, Table 1: Dimensions of Street-Level Leadership is presented. It depicts how four types of situations create differing types of challenges and opportunities for street-level public servants in exercising leadership: 1) those involving no substantial or limited discretion; 2) those involving choices about process; 3) those requiring decisions about outcomes; or 4) those demanding choices about process and outcomes.[1]

In quadrant 1, workers exercise little discretion in either the process or outcome dimensions; extant administrative rules effectively cover and structure behavior. Representative cases might

---

1. The model should not be interpreted as suggesting that discretion and leadership are related in a linear fashion, where more discretion leads to more leadership.

include teachers turning in grades at the end of an academic cycle or police officers notifying investigators and placing crime scene tape around the victim of an apparent homicide. Such circumstances can be anticipated by supervisors and policy makers, so rules and regulations can be developed to cover such situations. In Lipsky's (1980) terms, the variables in the human dimensions are minimal and the expected behaviors are predictable and simple. Thus, the actions of individual workers in such situations can be reduced to programmatic formats. Worker behavior in such contexts is not considered to be leadership.

In quadrant 2, street-level leaders exercise discretion over how to resolve a situation, but the specific goal they are to attain is relatively clear. Such situations might occur when a social-welfare worker must take custody of a child by court order or when a teacher must stop a fight. The outcome to be sought is known; however, the individual has choices over how to achieve the goal. In such cases, workers act as situational leaders; if the subject is resistant or uncooperative, it is appropriate to use highly directive action. However, if the subject is or becomes more cooperative and compliant, such use of power would be less legitimate and less effective. In such cases, effective workers operate as "situational" leaders.

In quadrant 3, street-level leaders have discretion over what outcome ought to be achieved, but little discretion over the process by which the goal is to be achieved once it has been chosen. Police officers, for example, exercise this type of discretion after they stop a suspected drunk driver. Because most officers do not carry in-car breathalyzers, they must decide whether the person ought to be arrested with incomplete information. Once they make the decision that a person is probably intoxicated, however, officer discretion is severely limited; they are obliged to arrest the person. Alternatively, if the officer decides the person is probably not intoxicated, the officer is obliged to let the person go. In doing so, the officer is making a decision based on the values of the community, balancing the need to protect the community from drunk drivers, while at the same time not wasting departmental resources or detaining a citizen if he or she is not drunk. That is, while the subject of arrest may not desire to be arrested, if larger social goals of order and safety can be seen to supersede the individual's desires, then the decision to arrest can be seen as legitimate. In contrast, if the decision to arrest is not made based on larger and broadly shared social values, but instead on ones like racial bias or personal enmity, that decision can be seen as illegitimate. In so acting, workers are exercising what we call "transformational leadership," enacting what Morgan (1990) calls "phronesis," Terry (1990) calls "conservatorship," and Kass (1990) describes as "stewardship."

Finally, quadrant 4 describes situations in which workers make discretionary choices about both the goals to be achieved and the means to reach them. Social-welfare workers who are called to a scene of apparent child abuse exercise this type of discretion when they make a determination of whether or not a child should be removed from a home and then how to handle the situation to accomplish this end. So do police officers when they decide whether to arrest the participants in a domestic dispute, and then determine what level of force and/or collaboration to use in resolving the situation. Importantly, both decisions—what to do and how to do it—can be explained and evaluated through reference to models of transformational and situational leadership. The decision to remove the child (or not) can be defended or criticized through reference to social, organizational, or moral standards. The means by which a removal (if chosen) is effected can be interpreted through a model of situational leadership. The legitimacy of both the goals and the means can be considered within the concept of street-level leadership as developed here.

Take, for example, the case that introduces this chapter. The worker clearly operated in what is defined as quadrant 4 of the model of street-level leadership. In the beginning of her investigation, the worker had to determine what outcome ought to be achieved in the case (i.e., should the children be removed or not; should the parents be referred for further services or not). These decisions were value-laden and almost necessarily were going to violate the expressed preferences of the parents, who, as the introductory description makes clear, thought they were being harassed and desired to be left alone to raise their children as they wished. Thus any decision to do anything other than leave the children in the home under their parents' control was going to place the worker in the position of a transformational leader whose decisions needed to be legitimated through reference to the broader community's norms, values, and expectations.

Additionally, the worker also made choices about how to achieve her goal once she established it. Unable to win immediate support from local prosecutors, she called on the local gas company and fire department to gain information and become, essentially, an "expert" on the dangers that the children would face if they remained in the home. She then used this expertise to persuade prosecutors to support her decision. She thus "led" the community by choosing a particular course for the situation, and then "led" the relevant actors by gaining their support for the decision.

As will be seen in the next chapter, the choices this worker made and the activities she undertook in support of her decisions are common to the workers studied in this project. Because such workers must exercise discretion, they do much the same things as those who are popularly considered "leaders" do. Additionally, because the concept of leadership requires legitimization through external norms and standards, it provides both a means to account for what workers do and the means by which their actions can be legitimated (or not). In exercising process and outcome discretion, workers can act as leaders, with all the potential and risk that the concept entails.

4

Leadership on the Street

The Work of Street-Level Public Servants: The Case of the Bruising Brothers

Police officers were dispatched to a domestic-violence call. When they arrived, they discovered that three adult brothers had been involved in an extensive shouting and shoving match, often in their front yard, for much of the evening. Neighbors had called to complain well after the fighting had begun.

The officers' first efforts were to establish order at the scene. The first officer to arrive was not able to physically separate the three brothers. Only after two additional officers arrived were they able to take each of the brothers to different parts of the yard. The officers began asking each of the men for his version of events. As the stories unfolded, the officers consulted with each other about what "the story" was.

As interviews commenced, it quickly became clear that the men were intoxicated. Two of the brothers admitted that they had been drinking beer all day. Further, the source of the argument slowly emerged: one of the brothers asserted that he owned the house as a gift from his mother and believed that his brothers were "trashing" it. The other men disputed their brother's ownership claim, insisting instead the home still belonged to their mother and that they were trying to get their brother to leave since he was the source of family diffi-culties. Each of the brothers accused another of assault, although none admitted to having done so and there were no apparent wounds on any of the men.

In the course of the interviews, the brothers continuously interrupted each other's stories, repeatedly making threatening gestures and comments. On more than one occasion, in fact, the brothers broke away from the officers who were interviewing them and moved toward each other, voices raised and fingers pointing. A large crowd of onlookers— some neighbors, some relatives who were called to the scene by one or other of the brothers—also gathered to watch the events. The officers, as a consequence, had to take actions both to keep the brothers separate and to control the crowd.

Once they had established reasonable control over the scene—a process which took at least twenty minutes and was never maintained for more than five—and had reviewed the apparent facts of the case, the officers began discussing what to do. They considered the fact that under the state's domestic violence law, they could place all three under arrest. As cohabiting relatives, the assault each of the participants claimed that the others had perpetrated gave them the authority to take all three to jail, resolving the incident for the night. However, they were explicit among themselves that they did not want to pursue arrest because they thought it would be a waste of time, money, and energy for a case involving three "stupid," intoxicated brothers who would never be prosecuted. On the other hand, they admitted that if it was necessary to end the fight, they would arrest all three men and put them in jail.

Having decided that they did not want to take the men to jail, the officers began exploring alternatives with the brothers. First, however, they made it very clear that unless the men cooperated, all three would go to jail. Initially, one of the brothers claimed he "didn't care" and insisted that he would "press charges" against the presumed troublemaker. A second brother, in contrast, immediately began begging the officers not to take him to jail since it would "ruin his chances to get on with the department," which was his "life-long dream" despite his admitted felony record. (When they heard this the officers smirked and, under their breaths, made derogatory comments about the man's potential for employment.) The third man steered a middle course, noting that there had not really been any punching in the fight;

rather, it was a "mutual wrestling match" which ended up on the floor in the kitchen. He also talked to his angry brother, trying to persuade him to be reasonable and keep the trio out of jail.

The officers also began working with the crowd of friends and relatives who had gathered to observe the incident. The officers allowed individual onlookers to talk to the brothers, and asked several if they would be willing to house one or other of the men for the night. They also asked the brothers if there was another place they could stay for the night so that the animosity among them might cool down. Finally, they got a commitment from one of the men to his brothers (the one the other two had accused of being the real trouble-maker) to move out the next day. That appeared to satisfy the participants and much of the anger began to dissipate.

Once they had found a place for the "odd man out" to stay, one officer drove the man to his friend's house and the other two officers returned to their regular patrol zones. From arrival on the scene until departure, the incident took approximately one hour and fifteen minutes.

INTRODUCTION

The argument that street-level public servants are, or can be, leaders may be theoretically interesting, but it is not relevant or terribly helpful unless it can be applied to the work they do. This chapter illustrates the four dimensions of street-level leadership outlined in Table 1 of the last chapter by applying them to some of the cases observed by the authors. It describes the choices and actions of the workers and explains how these behaviors were acts of leadership. It also examines the question of the legitimacy of worker choice making and how this question speaks to the reality of worker success and failure. As will be seen, street-level public service is often a complicated, contentious job, but its challenges provide opportunities for workers to exert leadership and serve the public by making their communities better places to live.

It should be noted that while we attempt to describe the components and applications of the model systematically and in some detail, the street-level leadership model is perhaps best understood as a *style of thinking*. Rather than providing a routinized or "canned" approach to decision making, it is intended to offer a different perspective or cognitive approach to defining situations and developing appropriate responses. Accordingly, the model is not intended to be used as a series of linear decision rules based on discrete categories. Instead, it is intended to provide a general framework for thinking about the kinds of choices that street-level public servants are called upon to make and how the legitimacy of their choices can be evaluated.

QUADRANT 1: ADMINISTRATIVE PROCEDURE

Quadrant 1 describes those activities over which workers exercise very little, if any, discretion. Administrative rules, supervisory standards, the law, and the like have adequately anticipated the relevant issues at play in a given situation and have prescribed routinized procedures that workers are to follow in such circumstances. As a consequence, workers have no real opportunity to act as leaders as defined in Chapter Three—except, perhaps, to recognize that they are in such a situation and so ought to follow the preestablished rules.

While completing routine paperwork and reporting requirements are the sorts of responsibilities commonly falling into this category, situations requiring little worker discretion are not necessarily insignificant. Perhaps the single most striking example of this type of situation was observed at the end of a police officer's graveyard shift, at approximately 7:00 a.m. The officer was called to the scene of a car on fire behind a local automobile dealer. As he neared the dealership, he could see thick black smoke rising over the building. He quickly drove to the area of the fire to hold back any crowd that might have gathered until local firefighters arrived.

The officer and the fire department arrived at the scene at roughly the same time, and while firefighters suppressed the flames shooting from a station wagon, the officer stood back and made a preliminary survey of the area. His first instinct, he said to the observer, was that it was an arson fire—caused either by "kids" or by someone with a grievance against the dealership. Indeed, once the fire was out and it was safe to approach the car, evidence of arson was apparent: a black trail of burned grass led from the car to a gasoline container lying empty on the ground.

After recognizing the fire as an arson, the officer took steps to secure the scene. As required by department rules, he ordered people not to get too close to the gas can so any fingerprints or footprints might not be disturbed, notified his supervisor of the fire, made sure that the fire department had called their arson investigator, and asked the dispatcher to notify someone at the dealership that one of their cars had apparently been set on fire.

Just as the officer was turning away from the gas can and was heading back to his car to wait for a relief unit (noting that he was already into overtime and his sergeant was trying to cut back on such time), one of the firefighters declared that the large lump that was visible in the front passenger's seat was a human body. (The lump was evident on a cursory inspection of the vehicle; however, it did not appear to be a body until a much more careful inspection was done.) The body was bent over, head in lap, arms by the side—indicating, the officer immediately declared, a murder instead of a suicide.

After first confirming the firefighter's statement, the officer's demeanor and behavior changed radically. He immediately ordered everyone at the scene—firefighters, a few onlookers, and the observer—away from the vehicle. He also established a broad perimeter around the site, later explaining that in their training officers who find bodies are told to "take as much territory as possible" to protect the scene, remembering that "you can always give it back later" if it is not needed. Additionally, he notified his supervisor of the apparent murder by land-line phone, again later explaining that officers were taught to use "real" telephones so that local news media and citizens with scanners could not learn of the incident right away. Finally, following established procedures, he took the names and personal information of everyone who had come near the car or had walked inside the boundary tape in order to provide this information to the homicide detectives when they arrived. He then stood within the boundary tape to prevent anyone from entering the scene and potentially disturbing evidence.

With these steps taken, the officer's role was largely complete. He had only to wait for detectives, for other patrol units to assist and then relieve him in controlling the scene, and to make sure that no unauthorized people went inside the tape. When relieved (approximately three hours after being dispatched to the call), he drove back to the station and went home. (The murder was ultimately solved, but that was another person's responsibility.) Department rules and norms had accurately anticipated the relevant variables under such circumstances and had established programmatic responses to them. The officer, then, did not really exercise leadership; rather, he served as a "bureaucratic" public servant, implementing rules and procedures with little personal interpretation or intervention.

Another observed case of a worker acting in accordance with administrative procedure with minimal discretion involved a social-service worker. The worker responded to a call from local police that a mother was refusing to allow a young teenage boy to return home. The boy was still at school and the police were requesting that she come to the school and drive the child to a shelter. When the worker arrived, the officer explained that he had interviewed the mother and that she had claimed that the boy was "out of control" and had hit his pregnant teenage sister in the stomach the night before. The police told her that they were not going to place the boy under arrest for assault and that the mother had stated that she would physically hurt the boy if he came into her home. The officer told the worker that the mother had said, "I don't want to end up like that mother who drove her kids into the lake, but I know I will hurt him if he comes home." Because the mother had stated her intent to inflict bodily harm on the child, the police could not release the boy to his mother. So, as was required by police department procedure, they called child protective services to get a worker to drive the boy to a shelter. In doing so, the child protective services worker exercised minimal discretion in determining either what would be done or how it would be accomplished. She simply provided transportation.

Other examples of how laws, rules, and norms shape worker actions could be discussed here. Whether it was social-service workers filling out forms every time they contacted someone or officers directing traffic at a busy intersection; whether it was child protective services workers responding to requirements that they investigate every claim of abuse or police officers filling out accident reports; bureaucratic procedures clearly shape what workers do and how they do it. Further, it is not always appropriate that workers exercise discretion—as was the case with the murder scene, worker discretionary choice making might lead to events that could undermine the integrity of the scene and thereby harm an investigation. However, as the other three dimensions of Table 1 suggest, such activities do not constitute the whole of street-level public service. It is to these other dimensions that this chapter now turns.

QUADRANT 2: SITUATIONAL LEADERSHIP

Quadrant 2 deals with those situations where the objective or outcomes to be sought are relatively set or structured (by the law, organizational routine, public pressure, and so forth) but the means to be employed for achieving those outcomes are not. Accordingly, street-level public servants have to make discretionary choices about how they work toward the expected goal. In such cases, they can be seen to act as situational leaders, and their actions can be evaluated with reference to such models.

One observed case of workers acting as situational leaders involved the removal of a child from a mother by direction of local prosecutors. On reviewing relevant material (the mother had already had one child removed from her home and had subsequently been reported for other apparent violations regarding her second child), local prosecutors decided that they were going to bring action in court to take custody of the infant. They decided, in essence, that the danger to the child was of a sufficiently high order that other values, such as keeping the family together, conserving limited tax resources, and the like, were subsumed under the need to protect the child. In support of this decision, they ordered that the department take immediate custody of the child. As a consequence, the worker in charge of this case had no discretion about the outcome; her only choice making had to do with how to fulfill the court's order.

The worker's department had a set of general policies and procedures to be followed in such cases. In compliance with these policies, the worker was accompanied by a coworker. Local police were dispatched to the scene, as was a local investigator who specialized in juvenile matters. The coworker explained that such precautions might seem excessive, but that the department had experienced troubles in such cases in the past and had experienced problems with the mother in this case.

While there were a number of agency rules and practices regarding such cases, there was still significant room for worker discretion in how the case would be handled. For example, the coworker explained that while ideally the mother would answer the door, the child would be at home, and the order could be quickly carried out, he also predicted that it would not be "that easy." Based on past experience, he said that even if the mother answered the door, she was likely to be argumentative and even violent. Alternatively, he predicted that either she would not answer the door or the child would not be at home.

It is worth noting here that, in contrast with the case of the officer who discovered the burned body in the car, there were no precise department rules about how the worker should deal with a reluctant client. Moreover, workers were not trained to handle such cases in a particular way. Workers regularly talked about how their training concentrated primarily on how to fill out paperwork properly. Thus, workers were generally expected to figure out how to handle these types of cases on their own. As a result, the events that transpired in this and similar cases evolved out of the interaction among the clients, the workers, and the circumstances.

In this case, the worker's expectation that there would be difficulties proved to be correct. After first refusing to answer the door, the mother did let the workers in. But the child, she said, was not at home, and she refused to tell workers where he was. She also became verbally abusive about a worker who was not present but who, the mother claimed, had caused all her problems. Throughout the woman's tirade, the worker in charge of the case continually worked with her, trying to persuade her to tell where the baby was. The worker explained that only by complying with the court order could the mother expect to have her child returned in the future and tried to draw the mother into a conversation about what steps she could take to ensure that there were no further incidents like the one at hand.

After approximately ten minutes of conversation and argument, the two department workers at the scene went into another room to discuss their options with the police investigator. The investigator explained that the mother's failure to comply was a crime and that he would arrest her if they wanted him to. After a brief discussion, the workers decided that arrest, or at least the fear of arrest, was their only option, and asked the investigator to proceed to arrest the mother. As the officer informed the mother that he was going to arrest her, she immediately confessed that the child was at her aunt's house. After extracting a promise from the mother that she would not call her aunt as the workers drove to her address, the workers then left for the child's reported location.

When they arrived at the aunt's house, it quickly became clear that the mother had lied. The aunt was asleep, having just arrived home from her job, and had no idea what the workers were talking about. (The police searched the woman's apartment with her permission in order to confirm her statement.) So, after apologizing for waking her up, the workers started on their way back to the mother's home to arrest her.

Along their route, the police investigator spotted the mother's car, stopped it, and arrested her. After arriving at the police station, the workers promised the mother that they would not press charges if she told them where the baby was. The mother agreed, admitting that the child was at her grandmother's house. The workers went to the location, found the baby, and took custody. The mother was then released.

At least two questions emerge from this story: 1) how is what occurred "leadership"? and 2) how can leadership theory account for the legitimacy of the worker's actions? In many ways, of course, these two questions proceed together, but it is analytically useful to consider them separately. As to the question of how what these workers did is "leadership," the answer can be developed along two dimensions. The first is in accord with the description of leadership offered in Chapter Three: Leaders are those who influence others and take actions toward legitimate goals. Within this frame, the worker in charge was clearly making decisions intended to achieve the objective established by the local prosecutors. She was the central actor in the matrix of individuals associated with the case; other people either assisted or resisted, complied with or challenged the worker's authority. Functionally, then, she was the leader on the spot.

The worker can also be seen to have exercised leadership in making choices about how the goal of taking the child into custody would be accomplished. As was discussed in Chapter Three, leaders engage in a number of behaviors as they work to achieve their goals: issue clarification, development of support, participation, direction, and the like. The worker in this case was observed to use a wide variety of strategies in response to changing circumstances. For example, using the terminology of the Hersey and Blanchard model (1988), when she first arrived at the house and the mother appeared to be compliant, the worker "sold" the mother on the importance of following the court order and then "participated" with her in trying to define a long-term solution to the problem after the child was removed. When these behaviors failed to win the mother's acquiescence, the worker "told" the mother to comply by working with the local detective to have her arrested. Finally, after the woman was actually in custody, the worker again "sold" and "participated" with the mother on the outcome at hand, finally winning support from her—and the truth as to the child's location. Each of these choices was an example of situational leadership, in that the worker chose different strategies based on the circumstances at hand in order to achieve her goal.

Not only can the choice of specific behaviors be seen as leadership, the legitimacy of those actions can also be addressed within leadership theory. As was discussed in Chapter Three, situational leadership models assume that leaders' effectiveness depends on understanding the needs and preferences of the constituencies to which they are accountable. At one level, this means that if a client is compliant, highly forceful action may achieve a leader's goal; such behavior is, in fact, inappropriate and illegitimate. Alternatively, if a client resists the leader's efforts, supportive and participatory strategies will be both ineffective and illegitimate. At another level, this means that the leader–follower relationship should be maintained and enhanced by the leader's actions. Accordingly, legitimacy is based on engaging in behaviors and making choices that are consistent with the requirements of the situation.

In this case, the worker's actions can be seen as legitimate relative to the options available to her and given the situational variables at hand. She assessed the situation as it evolved and used approaches that "fit" with the circumstances. When the mother was being compliant, she responded appropriately by supporting her and not attempting to coerce her behavior. On the other hand, when the mother refused to cooperate in locating the child, the worker became very directive because doing so was necessary to accomplish a legitimate objective.

Further, it can be argued that the worker's style was likely to enhance the broader relationship the client had with the department and the other social-service agencies with which she worked (police, other support agencies, foster parents, and so on). The worker's choice to address the client's anger toward another worker and her choice not to press charges against the mother once the child was found both seem more likely to improve the client's image of the department than a more directive, argumentative style would. On another dimension, the worker's cooperation in the mother's arrest seems likely to enhance the worker's reputation with the police department as a serious, effective worker. Finally, the fact that the child was removed from the home while these other goals were being achieved suggests that the worker's actions were effective and legitimate.

However, the legitimacy of the worker's actions might be questioned, particularly in hindsight. If, for example, the worker and police officer had arrested the mother immediately and not left her at the home, they might have saved time and public resources. But given the information available to the worker at the time, it was not possible to predict how the situation would turn out. If the mother had been arrested but the child had later been found at the aunt's home, that arrest and associated costs could also be interpreted as an unnecessary use of public resources. So given the circumstances and the information available, the worker's actions can be considered legitimate even though the case did not evolve in an ideal manner. As Jackman (1993) points out, legitimacy is not an all-or-nothing concept. Accordingly, in trying to understand whether workers take legitimate actions, it is necessary to recognize the circumstances they face and the values that inform their actions. In any case, the worker acted as a situational leader, and the appropriateness of her actions can be evaluated as such.

As to the larger question of the legitimacy of the decision to remove the child from the home in the first place, there is nothing in either the worker's leadership or models of situational leadership that can speak to this issue. In circumstances such as these, it is outside a worker's rights and abilities to meaningfully judge the legitimacy of the goal. The worker did, in fact, agree with the decision; however, had she not done so, she would still have been obliged to follow prosecutors' orders—their authority superseded her own, and eliminated her discretion about the outcome of the case. Similarly, despite the fact that the mother rejected the legitimacy of the pending court case, the other agencies and workers involved supported it and justified their actions in terms of its requirements. In such circumstances, then, workers behave as situational but not transformational leaders, and their actions and decisions need to be considered in light of this position.

There were many other cases of workers-as-situational-leaders observed during the research for this project. A second example is much like the first in that it involved taking custody of a child, but the circumstances were different. A young (28-year-old) mother was in the hospital after giving birth to her seventh child. All of her other children had been taken from her because she had neglected and abandoned them. The worker explained that the mother was a drug addict and an alcoholic, had been unable to maintain a consistent arrangement for housing, and the most recent baby, like her brothers and sisters, showed signs of fetal alcohol syndrome. The court had ordered that the baby be taken into custody before the mother left the hospital.

When the worker arrived at the hospital, the mother was lying quietly with her baby. The worker asked the mother if she knew why the worker was there. The mother said that she knew that the worker was there to take her baby. The mother did not seem angry, only sad. The worker asked the mother if she would like to get the baby ready for the trip. The mother proceeded to change the baby's diaper and asked if she could put her in the car seat. The worker said yes, and as the mother did so, she began to weep. The worker reminded her that if she could clean herself up and find a stable place to live, they could work together to reunite her with her baby. The mother nodded and said, "But I don't even have a picture." The worker then took the baby out of the car seat, carried her to the nursery, and had her picture taken, a process that took about fifteen minutes. She took the picture to the mother, let her say good-bye to the baby, and left.

In this case, the worker, in response to the mother's coopera-tion, used a very supportive approach. She allowed the mother to participate in the process as much as possible. While she certainly was not required to have the baby's picture taken, she explained that she felt a responsibility to support the mother's relationship to the child and that fifteen minutes was a small investment. She said that sometimes people turn their lives around and she said she wanted to give this mother and baby every chance, despite her dis-mal record in the past. Doing so, she said, in no way detracted from her objective of taking custody of the child. The manner in which she did so, she explained, was intended to accomplish other purposes in support of the child and mother.

In taking these actions, this worker's behavior can be inter-preted and legitimated as an act of situational leadership. As in sit-uational leadership models, she provided only that which was needed. Additionally, her decisions to have a picture of the baby taken and to offer a hope of the baby's return to the mother all embodied an appreciation of the mother's needs and preferences. They also maintained open lines of communication with the mother, thereby enhancing the leader–follower relationship. Finally, it achieved the worker's goal. This is the essence of effective, legitimate, situational leadership.

Still another example is related in the case described in the Preface to this book: the case of the police officers charged with removing an abusive female from a motel. As was explained, a local motel manager called police to remove a woman who had been swimming in the motel's pool fully clothed and had been verbally abusing guests. The law granted property owners the right to refuse service or accommodation to uninvited guests; as a consequence, the officers were required to get the woman off the motel's grounds. The question was how they would do so.

When they arrived at the motel, the officers discovered that the woman had entered a room (without permission); they followed her into the room to request that she leave. She refused, picking up the phone and sitting on the bed in defiance of the officers' orders. At that point, three officers entered the room and tried to escort her out. As soon as one of the officers touched her arm, however, the woman began fighting—kicking, flailing her arms, and pulling herself away from the officers in the room.

In the face of her opposition, the officers rushed the woman, wrestled her to the bed, and handcuffed her. They pulled her from the room and placed her in a patrol car. Then, when she began kicking the windows of the vehicle in an apparent attempt to escape or to express her anger and frustration, the officers pulled her from the car and bound her by her hands and feet behind her back—interrupted only by the arrival of the woman's husband on the scene. The officers then returned her to the car and drove her to jail.

What makes this case one of situational leadership instead of a straightforward case of application of administrative rules regarding the use of force may not be immediately obvious. As related, the case seems to be almost a textbook example of police employing force in ever-increasing measure in response to the client's behavior—actions that the department has trained and the law empowers officers to take. Why, then, can these officers be seen to have exercised "leadership" instead of applied bureaucratic rules?

First, like the social-service worker whose actions were described in the first case, the officers on the scene were clearly leading the group involved in this case. It was their choices, framed by the motel owner's demands that they remove the woman from his property, that shaped the events on the scene. Functionally, this put the officers in a position of leadership aimed at achieving the predetermined goal.

Further, the officers did apply the departmental rules in the case at hand. It wasn't that their leadership was separate from their organization's policies and norms. Rather, it was their approach to the case and the terms through which it can be legitimated that establishes their actions as those of situational leaders. For example, in their initial contact with the woman, only one officer entered the room to try to persuade her to leave. This action was reasonable given the woman's demeanor and, had it been successful, would have led to the quick and effective resolution of the case. However, when this attempt failed, the officer did not continually repeat his failed strategy; instead, he enlisted the help of the other officers. As a group, then, they entered the room in order to establish a more forceful control over the scene. Having achieved this control, they escalated their use of force by binding her arms and legs only as necessary in order to gain her compliance. In other words, the officers adopted approaches that seemed most likely to achieve their goal and adjusted these approaches as circumstances changed. This is, as was described in Chapter Three, the essence of effective situational leadership.

Interestingly, the officers were self-critical once the incident was over and the woman was fully in custody. During the drive to the jail, one of the officers expressed serious concerns over the outcome of the case, wondering whether the woman "needed" to go to jail or whether she could have been talked out of the situation if they had been more patient. In later conversations with the other officers involved, however, the officer learned that the woman had assaulted the first officer to approach her. Under those circumstances, the consensus among the officers was that the arrest was "fine" (i.e., that it was legitimate within the department's rules, culture, and the community's laws). It is also significant that the large crowd of onlookers who gathered in the motel parking lot where the arrest was made seemed to agree with the officers. Statements like "she's crazy" and "she just wouldn't listen" buzzed through the crowd, several of whose members made a special point of making the comments to the observer. Additionally, the woman's husband—who, as was explained in the Preface, appeared at the scene late in the fight and almost joined it—stated to the observer that he thought her arrest was legitimate once he found out that his wife had fought with the police. The officer, then, legitimated his work through reference to the circumstances of the situation, arguing that force was used only in the proportion necessary for achieving the required goal. This is the essence of legitimate situational leadership. In both action and evaluation, then, officers can be seen as leaders in this case.

But again, legitimacy is not an all-or-nothing concept. Some may object to the officers using what they may consider to be excessive force. Others may object that it would have been quicker and easier simply to forcibly arrest the woman from the start. Suggesting that the officers' actions were legitimate relative to the situation and the available alternatives does not mean that the actions taken necessarily worked as planned, or that no one would object to their decisions. Rather, it suggests that the officers' decision-making process reasonably considered the law, the presence of bystanders, and other situational factors; reflected an attempt to match their approach with circumstances as they developed; and accomplished the objective.

Another police case of situational street-level leadership was another motel incident. Two officers were dispatched to a complaint call about a loud party at a motel. The management, as was their right under the law, asked the officers to remove the partygoers from the premises. Thus, the goal was clear—the officers were required to remove the offenders. A number of strategies could be employed, however, to accomplish this task.

When the officers arrived at the room where the loud party was being held, they were confronted with people who were unwilling to cooperate. Loud music could be heard through the door, but when the officers knocked and tried to gain entrance, the offenders opened their door, recognized that they were faced by the police, and then attempted to close the door on the officers. In response, the officers pushed through the door and immediately began telling the protesting partygoers that they were going to be evicted and might be going to jail if they continued to resist the investigation. When the suspects began to insist that the police had no "right" to enter "their" room, the officers first told the clients to be quiet and then explained the law as it related to cases such as these. These actions changed the suspects' demeanors; they began to explain that they had taken the room for the night in order to "sleep it off" after their prom night celebrations and admitted that they had been "partying" a little too aggressively.

As the officers talked with the suspects, they also searched the room. In the course of their search, they found a small plastic bag with what appeared to be marijuana in it. Not only did they have to evict the room's residents, then, they also had to determine who to arrest for possession of a controlled substance. (Again, the outcome of the case was required under the law; the question was how to achieve it.) The officers announced that by law, they could arrest everyone in the room where the marijuana was found, but admitted that they did not want to do this. Such arrests, they explained to the observer, would be a waste of time and would require the investment of too much money and effort on a misdemeanor offense. However, they did want the person responsible for the presence of the drug to be held accountable. As a consequence, they asked whose marijuana it was, and when the man who rented the room declared that it was his, he was arrested. His friends were allowed to leave after quickly gathering their belongings.

With both of the situations described, the concept of situational leadership fits what these officers did quite usefully. First, the officers' discretion over what ought to be done was highly constrained; the motel owners required that the officers remove the residents of the room, and the law and departmental practice compelled the arrest of those in possession of marijuana. Second, the officers were clearly the primary actors on the spot. It was their choices, attitudes, and desires that directed the course of events. Third, the officers used a variety of behaviors and actions, ranging from more to less directive and more to less cooperative, including agenda setting and issue clarification, to achieve their goals. Finally, the legitimacy of their actions can be assessed in light of the objectives toward which they were acting. The residents were removed from the room, the person responsible for the marijuana was arrested, and the officers were able to return to their regular patrols without excessive use of force or substantial wasting of the department's time or of society's resources.

A final case of observed situational leadership involved a social-service worker who needed to make a follow-up call on a case of parental neglect. A woman had previously had two children removed from her custody, and while she subsequently had two more children, she was currently engaged to and living with a man who had a long history of physical and sexual child abuse.

The department had required her to separate from the man under threat of losing her children, and the worker had to investigate to make sure that this order was being complied with.

When the worker arrived, she found that the client was very confrontational. She said that she was very upset with the department for requiring her to live apart from her fiancé and insisted that he would cause no problems in the home. Further, the woman, who was very large, flung her hands in the air and otherwise appeared to try to intimidate the worker. (In fact, the worker had explained before going to the apartment that she was intimidated by the woman and might not have visited the woman had there not been someone else along, in this case the observer.)

The worker's response to this situation was interesting. Rather than confronting the woman, the worker attempted to de-escalate the obvious anger and tension her visit seemed to be provoking. She said she just wanted to "clear things up" so that the man could eventually return to the home. Since the main purpose of the visit was to ensure that the man had not yet moved back into the apartment, the worker did not engage in any detailed conversation about the man's history. Instead, she discussed the man's living status with the woman and reminded her of the importance of her complying with the department's order. The worker also noted that she would recommend that the man receive counseling for his anger and abuse problems before returning to the home. She then left.

Again, the concept of situational leadership can account for both what the worker did and the legitimacy of her actions. Like the workers in the other cases, this worker's choices and actions shaped events at the scene. Her decision to visit the client, her decision to de-escalate the situation, her decision to try to convince the client to follow the department's order, and her decision to recommend counseling for the father all shaped events in particular ways. Moreover, the worker utilized available resources—the department's ruling, her institutional position, the woman's expressed desire to see the return of her children and her fiancé to her home, and, for that matter, the presence of an observer—to accomplish her goal. Additionally, she matched her style to the situation at hand to the same end. Rather than meeting aggression with aggression, a strategy that seemed likely to cause a conflict that would lead to further unnecessary problems with the woman, the worker chose to work with the client on the client's terms. In doing so, the worker seemed to establish a foundation of trust with the woman and also fulfilled her responsibility. Within the broader framework of the department's decision, the statutory requirement to keep families together whenever possible, and the rights of clients, the worker's actions embodied the legitimate and effective exercise of situational leadership.

QUADRANT 3: TRANSFORMATIONAL LEADERSHIP

Street-level leadership can also involve discretionary choices about what goals or outcomes will be sought in a particular circumstance. In such circumstances as described by quadrant 3 of Table 1, workers can act as "transformational" leaders. They make choices and take action to elevate the goals, attitudes, and values of the participants in a given situation in ways that may be counter to their immediate interests and desires, but that can be legitimated through reference to the broader complex of ideals and values involved in the case.

One common type of police officer decision making that clearly fits quadrant 3 was arrests made for driving while intoxicated/driving under the influence (DWI/DUI). For several reasons, such arrests were observed to be among the most contentious and complicated which officers regularly confronted. First, citizens almost inevitably denied that they were intoxicated (in at least half of all cases, in fact, the driver claimed to have had precisely "two beers"). Second, more often than not such arrests were observed to involve citizens who were generally more familiar with the law and their rights than were other individuals. Thus, when officers explained the very technical law and court interpretations regarding drunken driving, it provided these clients with substantial opportunities for challenge. Additionally, while officers generally said that they thought drunk driving was a serious problem and admitted that they received administrative merit for making such arrests, they complained about the time and energy such arrests took, given that DWI/DUI was a misdemeanor offense. As a rule, workers claimed that their time could be better spent checking buildings and intervening in major crimes rather than meeting the specific requirements of a DWI/DUI law so that an arrest would not be overturned in court. From their perspective, then, a DWI/DUI arrest was a troublesome prospect.

While patrolling one night, for example, an officer spotted a car pulling out of a parking lot without its headlights on (a sign of driving under the influence). The officer followed the vehicle for some time, observing that the driver never turned his headlights on, had his car wandering within his lane (another sign of intoxication), and was driving slightly *below* the speed limit (another criterion for drunk driving). After observing the driver for about a mile, the officer stopped the vehicle and began his DWI/DUI investigation.

The driver immediately claimed that he was not intoxicated; instead, he admitted only to the ubiquitous "two beers." Further, he claimed that he had not turned on his headlights because the road was well lit and he "forgot." Finally, he explained his lane wandering by insisting that his car, which was an older model, was out of alignment.

The officer listened to the man's explanations, examined the car for open containers of alcohol (there were none), and began a standard battery of DWI/DUI tests with the driver. The man's speech was slurred, his breath smelled of alcohol, and he failed the field sobriety tests of balance and coordination. As such, the driver demonstrated several of the standard indicators for suspicion of DUI. As required by law, the officer informed the man of his rights, arrested him, and transported him to jail.

The arrest process of this driver did not end at this point. Instead, there was a formal set of requirements that the officer had to fulfill to complete the arrest. The officer took the man to the jail's DWI/DUI testing facility so that a formal breathalyzer exam could be administered. He also had to fill out extensive paperwork documenting the circumstances under which he stopped the driver, the driver's performance during the field sobriety tests, and his demeanor during the testing process. This examination and processing took an additional forty-five minutes, simply because the driver could not or would not blow into the machine with enough force for the machine to register his blood alcohol level. Throughout this procedure the driver kept insisting that he was innocent; that he would sue the department; that he did not think his tax dollars ought to be used arresting "guys driving home" when "real criminals" go free. However, when he successfully completed the test, the driver's blood alcohol level was well in excess of the legal limit, so he was finally booked into jail.

Once the driver was in jail and the officer headed back out on patrol, he explained his actions in terms that reflected both his status as a transformational leader and the constraints that he faced. The officer made it clear that he was very uncomfortable with the amount of time that the arrest had taken. He said he would have preferred to spend more of the time patrolling his assigned territory. He also admitted that the underlying logic of the driver's complaint—that time spent arresting him was time not spent catching "real" criminals—was true. However, he also said that he had seen too many accidents involving drunk drivers and had dealt with too many of the tragic consequences. Thus he felt comfortable with his arrest—he thought the driver "needed" to be arrested. The fact that the man protested was insignificant, given the other statutory, moral, and community interests at stake. His complaint, rather, was with the detailed and precise constraints on his behavior once the decision to arrest was made. Like transformational leaders, then, the officer acted toward a set of goals that were inherent to the broader community, even though those values were not immediately shared by the individual with whom he was working. His decision reflected a consideration of the need to be accountable to the law, the department, the community, and even to the man he arrested.

Another example of officers employing transformational leadership in a manner that limited their procedural discretion was observed when officers were called to a scene of a reported unlawful imprisonment. A woman reported that her daughter was prevented from returning home by the mother of one of the daughter's friends. The friend's mother, the friend, and the daughter all claimed that the mother had a history of alcoholism, regularly drove while intoxicated, and so argued that the daughter should not be released to her custody. In opposition, the mother claimed that her daughter had done badly on her schoolwork and so did not want to face punishment at home.

The officers thus had to balance competing claims of moral superiority and ethical responsibility in creating a solution to this incident. They had to weigh the mother's rights in parental authority with the daughter's right to be safe from abuse or threat. They also had to judge the mother's current emotional and physical condition and the daughter's truthfulness. In short, like transformational leaders, they had to make value judgments about what outcomes or goals would be legitimate in this situation.

It is important to note here that the officers who responded to this call made it clear that there were no departmental rules, training manuals, laws, or other procedures covering such a situation. Other than saying that they thought it was their responsibility to resolve the dispute, the officers admitted there were no real constraints on their choice making. So long as they felt they could justify their actions within the broad parameters of the law, they could make whatever decision they preferred.

The solution the officers worked out in this situation points both to the value-based character of the decision they made and to the way this decision constrained their choices of how to achieve the chosen outcome. The officers took the claim of the mother's alcoholism seriously and discussed it with her. They made it clear to her that if they found her to be intoxicated they would not return her daughter to her. Instead they would call the local child protective services agency and ask them to take custody and to initiate an investigation of the mother. They also explored the question of whether the daughter was likely to be abused by talking to the mother, the daughter, and the friend's mother. In short, they explained to the observer that they were exploring whether they were required under the law or otherwise felt it imperative to remove the child from the mother in order to protect the girl's safety.

As the officers explored these questions they discovered that, while the mother admitted she was an alcoholic, she was not currently intoxicated. They also found that there was no reported history of abuse in the family. As a consequence, they decided that there were no grounds on which they could justify removing the girl from the mother's custody. They did say that had the mother been intoxicated they would have decided differently, and they told the mother this as they urged her to get help for her problem. However, since there was no immediate threat to the child's wellbeing, they ordered her returned to her mother.

Like transformational leaders, then, the officers who handled this call had to weigh competing claims of moral authority in deciding what was the best outcome for this case. Many different standards might be applied in making this judgment: the need to keep families together versus the need to protect children; society's interests in helping families deal with their problems versus the need to protect an individual's rights; and so on. Regardless of what choice they made, then, the officers' decision could be criticized. In fact, neither the mother, the daughter, the friend, nor the friend's mother was pleased with what the officers did. However, the officers argued that this solution was legitimate according to the community, social, legal, and moral standards relevant to the case. As such, they behaved as transformational leaders behave, and standards for evaluating the legitimacy of their choices can be derived from the concept.

Social-service workers, too, regularly make judgments about what the right outcome for a case is that nonetheless limit their process discretion. One typical case involved a report of potential child abuse and neglect that was assigned to a social-service worker for investigation. The anonymous reporter alleged that the parents regularly fought, that they allowed their young children to run in the road, that the mother was running an unlicensed daycare, and that their children were locked in their rooms for extended periods of time.

Again, it is worth noting that there were no precise guidelines in the form of departmental rules, laws, or procedures about exactly how the worker was to resolve this case. While child abuse is a crime and workers are trained to recognize signs of abuse in both children and adults, there are no hard and fast rules that govern the determination of abuse in all cases. Instead, it is often the case that abuse manifests itself subtly, so workers have to assess it in specific instances. It is based on these assessments that workers make judgments about what ought to be done and why.

When she arrived at the home, the worker identified herself and explained the purpose of her visit. The mother unhesitatingly let the worker in, and responded in apparent shock and surprise to the allegations. She immediately offered to allow the worker to inspect her home and explained that she thought the report was a result of a dispute that she and a neighbor had been having with a third area resident. She also said that she had contacted the department and other officials about receiving an in-home daycare license since she did babysit a number of children every day. Finally, she admitted that she had placed childproof door handles on the inside of the door to her son's room because he was developmentally disabled and she wanted to prevent him from sneaking out of his room during the night. She insisted, however, that she never left the boy alone in the house, and explained that her five-year-old daughter was able to work the handles in case of emergency.

After talking with the mother, the worker talked to her two children without their mother present. The younger, developmentally slow child was able to provide very little information. However, the woman's five-year-old daughter largely confirmed the mother's story about why there were childproof handles on some doors. She also said that her parents did not hit or otherwise improperly touch her or her brother.

Once she had completed her interview, the worker then asked to inspect the house. On her tour, she recommended that the childproof door handles be removed so that they would not pose a problem in case of emergency. The mother immediately agreed. The worker also told the woman that the locking mechanism the family used to keep a pantry door closed was a potential hazard; the woman's husband immediately removed the device and put it in the trash.

At the end of her visit, the worker told the family that she would close the case and "unfound" the report. Accordingly, she had no process discretion, since the decision to unfound the case meant that she had no right to do anything else. However, she did explain that the family could call the department and ask that their file not be shredded so that they could start a harassment file against the neighbor they thought reported the incident. She then left.

It could be argued at this point that calling what this worker did "transformational leadership" is a bit of a stretch. After all, in one sense, she did not *do* anything except decide not to act in a case where the evidence did not obviously support any alternative choice. There are at least two reasons, however, why it is useful and appropriate to view the worker's actions as "leadership" rather than a straightforward application of bureaucratic rules. First, it is the essence of transformational leadership that the leader's decisions are based on the "true" (within the leader's understanding of them) wants and needs of followers. Transformational leaders, in essence, choose among competing visions of what ought to be done and derive legitimacy for their decisions within the broader community's values and ideals. In this sense, choice, even the choice not to take an action, is still an act of transformational leadership. Thus, the worker's choice to "unfound" the case was a choice in favor of the family and against the anonymous tipster. This choice was then supplemented by her suggestion to the family that they could begin a file in their defense against the neighbor.

Additionally, standards by which the worker's decision can be legitimated can be derived within the transformational leader concept. The law requires that children be left with their families whenever possible. However, the law also considers child abuse a major crime, and it is the organizational purpose of the worker's institution to enforce this value. Moreover, the law grants workers broad authority, indeed virtually police authority, to achieve their goals. Yet as profoundly as citizens want children protected, they do not want their tax money spent in support of inappropriate actions and they do not want children removed from home unnecessarily. So workers, whether they choose to remove children or not, have to justify their decision in relation to these broader ideals—just like transformational leaders in government, business, social organizations, and the like. In this case, the worker decided that the risk of harm to the children was extremely low and that no overriding social value would give her the right to remove the children from the home. This decision was informed by her understanding of what was legitimate within the boundaries of the law, the department's rules, and the community's expectations. The concept of the transformational leader, then, both describes what the worker did and embodies standards through which her actions can be evaluated. Accordingly, her actions placed her in the position of the transformational leader.

A somewhat more obvious case of a social-service worker acting as a transformational leader whose choices limited his discretion about process involved the placement of a child who had been taken from her mother at birth because the baby had cocaine in her system. The mother had previously admitted that she had used crack within two weeks of the baby's birth, and the child had been taken by the department the night before. The baby's declared father (the couple was not married), however, asked that he be given custody of the child. He said that he did not live with the mother, had no history of child abuse or other criminal activity, had no knowledge of his partner's extensive arrest record (mostly for prostitution and drug possession), and so wanted to have the baby in his home while the case was adjudicated.

Importantly, prior to meeting with the couple, the worker had done research into their records. In addition to the mother's record, the father, despite his claims, had several arrests in another county on various charges, as well as harassment charges in the local county. The father also had previously been charged by the department with inadequate supervision of another of his children, who had tested positive for drugs. The worker further checked the department's records and found that the couple had usually been found living together, regardless of the father's claims to the contrary. Finally, while the man insisted that he did not use drugs at all, in a previous contact the mother claimed that the father regularly used marijuana. In fact, the man appeared to be high on some drug other than alcohol in the interview.

When confronted with this information, the father claimed that he thought that the worker only was concerned with arrests in the local county and that he had forgotten about his harassment charge. He also said that the inadequate supervision charge had been illegitimate because the child had not been in his custody at the time of the incident. In any case, he insisted that his baby ought to be given to him while any court actions proceeded.

In light of the interview and the additional information he had gathered, the worker decided that he would not place the child with the father. In simple terms, the worker said that he thought both parents had lied to him in the interview and that he did not believe that the father really lived in an apartment separate from the mother. Given the father's criminal history and apparent child neglect, along with his belief that the parents were still living together, the worker denied the father's request for custody.

As with the previous cases discussed in this section, the worker in this situation can be seen as a transformational leader, both in terms of what he did and the terms in which his choices can be legitimated. Like transformational leaders, he chose among competing values and ideals to select the ones he thought were most appropriate under the circumstances. Then, it is through these values and ideals that his decisions can be legitimated. The value placed on protecting children from abusive situations, as expressed in the law and institutionalized in the agency for which he worked, led him to keep the baby out of the father's custody. The father disagreed, of course, but this disagreement only points to the nature of the choice making the worker faced: it was based on broad social wants and needs that ran counter to the father's wishes, but which manifested deeper ideals and values. Once the worker made the decision not to place the child with the father, however, his discretion was highly constrained. He had to leave the child in departmental placement. As such, this case fits quadrant 3 of Table 1. (Interestingly, the local newspaper reported that the mother and father were subsequently arrested for drug dealing in their shared apartment.)

A final example of transformational leadership involved a social-service worker investigating a report from a citizen claiming that an elderly woman in her neighborhood was no longer able to take care of herself, that homeless people were taking over her home, and that the woman should be placed in a residential facility. The worker explained to the observer on the way to the woman's house that there had been a long battle between the woman, her neighbors, and ultimately the city, over piles of garbage and debris that she had accumulated in her yard. After several years, the city had finally prevailed when they brought in a crew to clean up the mess and sent the woman a bill for the cost.

When the worker arrived at the home, the woman was lying on an old couch on her front porch drinking a bottle of soda. The house was unpainted and run down, but there was no garbage or other debris in the yard. When the worker approached, the woman sat up and asked the worker what she wanted. The worker explained that she was just checking up on her to see if she was all right. In response to the worker's questions, the woman explained that she had decided to live on her front porch. She showed the worker her hot plate and cans of food, and explained that a homeless husband and wife had been sleeping on her porch "to keep her safe." When asked where the couple was, the woman said that they generally went to the park in the morning to clean up and give her some privacy. When asked where she cleaned up, the woman explained that she used the bathroom in the house, but that she didn't go in there very often. Overall, she appeared suspicious and slightly hostile, but coherent. The worker asked her several times if she needed or would accept any kind of assistance with meals, housing, or other services. The woman was adamant in her refusal.

The worker asked if she could look inside the woman's home to make sure everything was okay. The woman narrowed her eyes and said no. The worker kept talking to the woman and attempted to convince her to allow her to look in the house. The woman finally said, "I will if you promise not to report me. Do you promise?" The worker said she would not report on anything she saw that day. The woman agreed.

The house was literally filled, floor to ceiling, with garbage, assorted articles, "collections" of sorts, and debris. A narrow passageway led to and through the bathroom, to the kitchen, and to the bedroom. Otherwise, every other space was filled. There was a huge pile (about seven feet across) of old shoes, mounds of news-papers, stacks of wood, a corner filled with rotting refuse, bottles, old linens, boxes and boxes of plastic flowers and knickknacks, dishes, food containers, but mostly just bags of rotting garbage. If there were any pieces of furniture or appliances, they were not visi-ble because of the clutter. The worker tested to see if the water worked in the bathroom. It did. The woman said, "I want you out now." The worker and observer went back outside. The woman appeared to grow angry. The worker gently told her that they needed to talk some more about her house next time she visited, and left.

The worker had several options available to her in determining what she wanted to accomplish in this case. First, she could recom-mend that the woman be declared incompetent and proceed with legal arrangements to put her under the care of a legal custodian or guardian and have her placed in a residential facility. Second, she could report the home to the fire department and have it declared a fire hazard, thereby forcing the issue of either cleaning it up or moving out. Third, she could close the case because the woman was an adult with the right to refuse services, because she was apparently capable of feeding and caring for her basic needs, and because she appeared to be coherent. Fourth, she could keep the case open for a while to see if the situation deteriorated and to try to convince the woman to change her living situation one way or another.

After some consideration, the worker decided on the fourth option, to keep the case open for a while. Her reasoning was based on a balance of factors and considerations. The worker explained that the woman probably would not do well in a residential facil-ity, in part because she would have to be forced to go. Second, although the neighbors were uncomfortable with the woman's life-style choices, she was basically caring for herself. The relationship between the woman and the couple that she allowed to sleep on the porch with her seemed relatively stable and had not, to this point, seemed to have posed any immediate danger. She said she thought that while the house might pose a fire danger, the woman was not sleeping in the home and the structure was far enough away from neighboring homes to make it unlikely that a fire would spread. The worker also pointed out that the woman was an adult, not a child, and that in our society we value adults being able to make choices for themselves even if others consider those choices to be unwise. She said she felt her supervisor would support her decision. Maybe most importantly, the worker said, "I want to build her trust." The worker explained that she did not expect the situation of camping on the porch to last indefinitely, and that she wanted to have a relationship with the woman so that perhaps she would allow the worker to help her at some point. "I'm afraid," she said, "that if I force this situation and we move her, she will not do well." If helping the woman was the overall goal, she said, then this was the best course of action.

In making this choice, the worker was acting as a transformational leader. She considered both the stated and unspoken needs and wants of the woman in the context of other competing values, expectations, and norms. She made her decision in a way that elevated and advanced community values in a manner that was consistent with the need to position herself to help the woman, protecting both her safety and her rights, and satisfying broader values about choice. As such, her decision can be argued to be legitimate, even though the woman was not immediately pleased with her involvement and her neighbors may have been unhappy that the woman was not simply taken away.

QUADRANT 4: TRANSFORMATIONAL AND SITUATIONAL LEADERSHIP

Quadrant 4 deals with those situations in which street-level public servants have to make choices about both what ought to be done and how best to achieve the goal. In such cases, workers can be seen to act as both transformational and situational leaders.

One of the observed cases that fits into quadrant 4 was the case described in the introduction to Chapter Three about the children living in the dirty home with smoke and high carbon monoxide levels. As was discussed there, the worker investigating this case had to decide both what to do and how to do it. Moreover, the worker clearly acted as both a transformational and a situational leader in carrying out her decisions.

As a transformational leader, for example, the worker addressed a number of competing values as she made her decision. The parents expressed a clear preference that they wanted to be left alone to raise their children as they wished. There is both public sentiment and statutory law that expresses a strong preference to leave children in homes, especially when there is no serious risk of harm. Local prosecutors also voiced serious reservations about removing the children from the home. However, the worker's assessment of the situation caused her to conclude that the children were in immediate danger of serious health problems or even death from carbon monoxide poisoning. As a result, she decided that the need to take action to protect the children's safety outweighed other considerations in this case. Accordingly, she decided to pursue the removal of the children from the home.

Since she faced significant resistance, accomplishing this objective would require her to take several immediate steps. These steps were not only appropriate from a procedural standpoint, but also helped her to establish the legitimacy of her action to take custody of the children. For example, in contacting the local gas and fire departments to ask them to evaluate the safety of the home, the worker was gathering information that could be used to persuade others, particularly local prosecutors, to support her position. Such actions reflect her awareness of the multiple points of accountability she faced: the prosecutor's office, the law, the school, her personal and professional values, the children, the family, the community, and her department. Once she had weighed these factors and gathered the appropriate information, she also made the decision to stick with the case all day, refusing to let it go. Her persistence clearly shaped the outcome of the case.

As such, the legitimacy of her actions can be judged within the concepts of the transformational and situational leader. The substantive values that the worker drew on to support her decision were based on the broadly shared idea that children should be protected from danger, as weighed against other interests and values in this particular case. The steps she then took to achieve this goal were both procedurally legitimate and effective.

Another case involving worker choices about both the goal to be sought and the best approaches to achieve that goal involved a social-service worker investigating a case dealing with a terminally ill woman and a potentially abusive or neglectful husband. The worker received a referral from a local hospital about a recently discharged female patient. The staff had observed the patient's husband repeatedly verbally assaulting and threatening his wife during her stay. The night before her discharge, the patient's husband had become so verbally abusive and out of control that security had been called to remove him from the facility. As a result, hospital staff were concerned for the safety of the woman at home and filed a report with the state social-service agency.

The intake report given to the worker stated that there was a family history of physical and emotional abuse. The report also stated that the woman's sons were willing to leave the home and move into an apartment with her and help take care of her. Under state law, the worker could intervene to force the separation of the husband and wife if it was determined that the woman was unable to care for herself and in immediate danger. However, he first had to decide whether to use this power or not. Then, in light of which decision he made, he would have to decide how to achieve this goal.

The worker made arrangements to talk with the woman that afternoon while she was receiving outpatient kidney dialysis. After introducing himself and explaining who he was, he asked her to tell him about the situation with her husband. The woman claimed that her husband was doing the best that he could. She stated that her sons could not move out, but was unable to explain why. When asked if she wanted help in getting away from her husband, she said no. She said that her husband loved her. She said, "He takes me to the doctor and fixes my meals—breakfast, lunch, and dinner. He's trying." When asked if he had been hitting her, she said, "He hasn't hit me for a long time, maybe five years. I got a protection order then. Now, he just gets mad and yells at me." The worker told her that the situation wasn't good for her medically and that the doctors were worried. She said, "You have to go soon so that he doesn't see you when he picks me up."

The first decision that had to be made was whether to pursue the matter or close the case. Either decision was defensible according to departmental policy. Importantly, however, the official department policy was that workers were to either close or "find" cases as quickly as possible. If a case was found to involve abuse or neglect of a vulnerable adult, the abused person would be removed from the situation and the case would be turned over to another social-service unit for ongoing services. This worker's job was simply to investigate the claim. In practice, however, he and his coworkers sometimes kept cases open for longer than usual when the circumstances were unclear or when the worker felt that to either close or find a particular case was inappropriate for one reason or another. Although such practices were officially frowned upon, there was an unspoken understanding that workers did so on occasion. Workers who did so consistently, however, were reprimanded both formally and informally.

In this situation, the worker decided to keep the case open for a while. In explaining why, he said that he wanted to see what developed over the next week or so before making a finding. Although the woman was claiming that her husband was doing his best, the observations of the hospital staff and the woman's physical vulnerability outweighed the woman's initial desire for him not to intervene. After all, he said, she might just be too afraid to ask for help. But, given that she would not admit to being abused and wanted to stay with her husband, he was hesitant to try to take immediate action. So, in this case, the worker made the decision to pursue the case based on his assessment of the needs and wants of the woman—her desire to stay with her husband, but also her unspoken need to be safe and taken care of. He noted that, as the woman had stated, the reports of physical abuse were more than five years old, and that the woman had demonstrated her willingness to use the legal system if necessary to protect herself. But, he said, the situation was serious enough and the woman was vulnerable enough that he could not simply close the case. In considering these competing values and needs, the worker acted as a transformational leader in crafting a solution that he felt best met those needs consistent with higher-level legal, institutional, and societal norms.

Having decided to keep the case open, he then had to make choices about how to pursue it. Given his assessment of the situation, he took a supportive approach, offering gentle direction when needed. He asked the woman if he could speak with her husband sometime soon. She said no. He explained that he would only tell her husband that he knew that he was doing his best and offer to get him some help in taking care of her and dealing with the anger and guilt he must feel about his wife's illness. He explained that it might even be possible to get a counselor to come to the house. Otherwise, he said, she might have to move out for her own safety. She was quiet for a while and then agreed to have the worker speak to her husband. The worker expressed support for her courage. The worker then left, promising to contact her husband later that day (wanting to avoid unexpectedly confronting him at the kidney dialysis center).

In making decisions and taking action to protect the woman and ensure her care, the worker behaved as a situational leader. He varied his approach with the woman, alternately supporting her and telling her the facts as indicated by her reaction to the worker and the situation. Given the information that he had, he decided to try to intervene with the husband first so that he could assess his willingness to receive outside assistance and support. He also noted that if the husband refused and the situation became dangerous, the woman could quickly be placed in a facility or with relatives. Cumulatively, the worker can be seen as acting as both a situational and transformational leader, evaluating and responding to situational factors while pursuing objectives based on a balance of values. Such actions embody the concept of effective leadership in that they clearly responded to the needs of the family in ways intended to enhance the leader–follower relationship across time and in ways that were likely to achieve the worker's goal of protecting the woman as fully as possible.

The case that begins this chapter provides a similar example of street-level public servants acting as both transformational and situational leaders. Under the laws of the state in which this incident occurred, it was within the legal rights of the officers to arrest all three brothers for domestic battery. However, the officers expressed serious concerns about simply exercising their authority in this way, since they thought the case probably would not be prosecuted and the brothers posed no real threat to the broader community. Even so, they realized that it was their duty to resolve the situation, at least for the night. Accordingly, they made a decision to separate the brothers, but not to place them under arrest. With this, the fight ended and the officers were able to resume their patrols.

Importantly, the legitimacy of these workers' actions can be evaluated within the transformational leader concept. The brothers, after all, did not want to go to jail, and indeed, did not really want the officers on the scene at all. Moreover, while the neighbors who called the police wanted the fight resolved, a number directly asked the officers not to take them to jail since the brothers were "just drunk." At a broader level, while it is clear that society considers domestic violence a sufficiently serious issue that many states have passed mandatory arrest laws, it is also the case that citizens do not want police officers to intrude too deeply into family affairs and do not want police departments to invest valuable resources in pursuit of suspects whose arrests will not be productive. And while departments review officers for arrests and other kinds of measurable activities, no department rewards offic-ers who spend hours working on a single, misdemeanor offense. The choice these officers made, then, was informed by their sense of what the most important values at hand were (i.e., their need to return to their patrol zones while controlling the incident for the night). As such, they were acting as transformational leaders, set-ting the broader community on a particular path with a set of con-sequences that were very different than might have been the case had they chosen another solution.

Additionally, the officers took steps as situational leaders, as they established and maintained control over the brothers, utilized friends and family members in achieving a resolution to the con-flict, and worked with the siblings to obtain their participation in overcoming the problem. Like situational leaders, they used a vari-ety of more and less coercive behaviors and tactics that supported their plans. Moreover, the legitimacy of their actions can be estab-lished within the broader framework of their choice of outcomes: they did not get excessively physical with the men, for example, nor did they simply stand by and let the men argue. Instead, they intervened, established goals, set priorities, and worked with the brothers, neighbors, and family members in a variety of ways in support of their goals. These actions were both effective and legiti-mate within the broader context of department procedures, social norms, and in the eyes of the witnesses at the scene. Even the brothers eventually indicated their support for the decision, with one volunteering to be driven elsewhere to spend the night.

Another of the observed cases that illustrates the concepts of transformational and situational leadership as they apply to line-level public service began when an officer stopped a car for speed-ing at approximately 2:00 a.m. When he looked in the vehicle, the officer discovered five occupants: four sixteen- to eighteen-year-old males and one female who gave her age as fourteen but looked younger. Other than the driver, none of these youths could be seen to have committed any legal violations; there were no open alco-hol containers in the car, nor was there any evidence of illegal drug use. As a consequence, there was no legal, coercive means by which the officer could end the late-night joy ride and send the teenagers home. Yet, at the same time, the officer expressed strong discomfort with the idea of a fourteen-year-old (or younger) girl riding around in a car at night with four older boys, and so was unwilling to simply ticket the driver and continue his patrol. The officer had, in sum, to balance his personal beliefs and community values about the moral "rightness" of removing (or not removing) the girl from the situation with concerns about the civil liberties of the car's occupants. He also had to decide how best to achieve his goal once it was established.

In deciding what to do, the officer was clear about the complexities in his decision making. For example, he expressed concerns that he would be shirking his duty if he took the time to drive the girl home. He also considered the possible consequences for the girl if she had an abusive home situation; in fact, the officer asked the girl if she thought she would be abused if he took her home, to which she answered that she thought she would. Finally, he considered the interests of her parents who, she admitted, did not know that she was out so late at night.

The officer also was quite explicit about the values he considered as he made his decision to drive the girl home. First, he admitted that, "If it were my daughter, I'd want her brought home." Riding around so late at night was, he said, "just wrong." Further, the officer stated that if he had let her go and then something had happened to her, not only could he not have forgiven himself, but he might have been held legally liable. Thus, he believed that there were legal and ethical pressures on him to take her home, even though no law or policy commanded that he do so. The officer also admitted that he felt comfortable taking her home on this particular night because it was relatively "slow," and so the time he spent involved in explaining her behavior to her parents would not unduly hinder the department in performing its duties. Finally, he considered the prospect of abuse by her parents and so left himself an "out" for his decision; if abuse was likely, he could protect her from her parents by removing her from the home.

In this situation, then, the officer decided that he would take the girl home. He ultimately decided that parental rights superseded the teenager's. However, he knew he had a range of alternatives about how he could accomplish this goal: he could drive her home and drop her off; he could follow the car and make sure her companions took her home; he could simply tell the driver to escort her home; or he could meet with her parents to explain the situation and assess their reaction in terms of the potential for abuse. He ultimately chose this latter course, promising her that he would stay with her as she explained the incident and that he would not leave her with her parents if it appeared she was likely to be physically assaulted. This course also guaranteed that she would get home as he desired.

When they arrived at the girl's home, the officer discovered that her parents were not at home, but an older sister was. He spoke with the sister at length, directly asking if the teenager would be abused once her parents got home. When she said no, that her parents never hit either of them, the officer left the girl at her home and reported that he felt he had done a good job; the parents would have a chance to correct the girl's behavior and other possible problems had been prevented.

In taking these actions, the officer acted as both a transformational and a situational leader: he employed standards based on departmental procedures, the law, and his assessment of the individuals directly involved in the case, as well as what he judged to be the broader community interests in protecting young people, to define what he thought was the right outcome. He then took steps that he thought would best achieve his goal: rather than trusting the driver to participate in the solution by driving the girl home unescorted, for example, the officer used a more directive approach and undertook the job himself. Further, he entered the girl's home prepared to use a variety of strategies that would protect her safety. He adopted the participatory approach when it became clear that the family would exercise what he thought was appropriate discipline against the girl.

Importantly, as with all the other cases, although the officer's decision can be justified as legitimate, objections can be raised. For example, it could be suggested that the officer was intervening in the personal lives of citizens rather than simply enforcing the law, as he is charged to do. He might be criticized for allowing his personal values to intrude on his decisions. He might be challenged for leaving his patrol zone for an extended period of time to handle a case that was not a problem by any legal standard and in which the girl was in no apparent risk either in the car or at home. These objections do not necessarily mean that the actions of the officer were illegitimate, however. Rather, these objections point to the fact that street-level leadership is complex, often involving choices that involve trade-offs and uncertainties. So in this case, as with many others, legitimacy is a relative concept, dependent on situational factors, the range of available options, and a balance of sometimes competing values. The worker's ability to think through these issues and make judgments that are defensible, not necessarily perfect, is the essence of leadership, whether situational, transformational, or both.

"FAILURE" AND LEADERSHIP ON THE STREET

Two challenges to the street-level leadership model might be raised at this point. The first is simply this: what gives these workers the right to weigh these values and make these kinds of moral judgments? Isn't it wrong that police officers, social-service workers, and others are making what amount to life-and-death decisions based on their own individual assessments of what values, norms, rules, needs, and expectations are most important in a particular circumstance? It is unsettling to think about the level of responsibility and power these individuals have. But questioning the rightness or wrongness of it largely misses the point. For the reasons outlined in Chapter Two, street-level discretion is inevitable. While the appropriate scope and nature of this discretion can be debated, the truth is that every day, in communities across America, public servants are making just these kinds of choices. We suggest that examining the legitimacy of these choices on a case-by-case basis is a far more constructive and positive approach than simply railing against their power. Moreover, it can be argued that these workers are ultimately in the *best* position to make these choices because of their vantage point from the street. Only they can see how situations unfold, and how seemingly similar circumstances can call for strikingly different responses.

It might also be objected that all of the stories related so far have been positive in the sense that the workers discussed were seen to make legitimate choices and act in effective ways. This argument is valid, at least to some degree, since most of the cases observed for this project *were* successful and legitimate and because the purpose of the earlier discussion was to illustrate the dimensions of Table 1. But no model of worker action can be complete unless it can account for inappropriate and illegitimate behaviors. Accordingly, this section deals with the concept of worker failure and discusses the ways in which it can be understood within the street-level leadership model.

There are at least three types of failure that can be seen to arise in the work of street-level public servants as leaders: failure of result or outcome, failure to use an appropriate style to achieve a particular goal, and failure to recognize what the appropriate goal is in a given situation. A fourth category, "uncertain," ought also to be introduced since there may be circumstances in which values change, making it very difficult to determine what constitutes the appropriate goal or action in a specific case.

Failure of result refers to those cases in which workers take what can be defended as legitimate, appropriate, and reasonable actions in accord with established departmental, legal, and other procedures and norms, and yet the case "goes sour." For example, a social worker may decide not to remove a child from his or her home because there is no clear indication that the child is in immediate danger. Or the court may order a worker to return a child home, and later the child is injured or killed. The worker may then be accused of failing to protect the child. Likewise, a police officer may stop a suspected drunk driver who subsequently passes a breathalyzer test. Under the law, the officer *must* release the suspect. But if that driver then gets into an accident and kills or seriously injures him/herself or another person, the officer can be said to have "failed" to protect the community at large.

At one level, such cases of "failure" are not failures at all, at least not at the worker's level. As has been noted throughout this book, workers are constrained by numerous external factors. A worker is only one actor in a matrix of influences. Sometimes rules, their organizations, the law, or other entities force them to take actions they would not otherwise choose. Alternatively, workers, however wise and insightful, cannot always be present when things are going wrong. As one social-service worker put it in describing a case, "The only way I can make absolutely sure that kids won't be hurt is to move in with them. The best I can do is to decide what I think is in their best interest based on the information I have."

On the other hand, such "failures" do matter in the work of street-level public servants for at least two reasons. First, if such incidents are made public, as they often are, it is almost always the case that individual workers are held at least partially to blame for what happens. Workers themselves made repeated references to this fact, complaining that citizens and the media did not understand the complex environment in which they did their jobs. This accountability, as was suggested in Chapter One, significantly influences the environment in which workers act because public pressures and expectations inevitably shape the law, department rules, and citizen supportiveness of or challenge to the legitimacy of worker actions.

Further, failures of outcome may result from failures of effective situational or transformational leadership. That is, it may be that a worker failed to utilize effective strategies to achieve a goal. Or a worker may not have had a sufficiently broad vision of what *might* be achieved in a case to define it in a creative, new way. In other words, the worker may not have had to take the undesired action if he or she more effectively defined the desired outcome or mobilized more support for it. While the "undesired" outcome may occur regardless of their actions, there may be resources available to workers as leaders that can help them to achieve their preferred goals.

Another type of failure that can be anticipated by and accounted for within the model of street-level leadership involves the failure to match an appropriate leadership style to a specific goal. In such cases, the outcome to be sought is clear and steps must be taken to accomplish it. In contrast with the stories related earlier in this chapter, workers might act in ways that do not help them to achieve their goals or are inappropriate for the situation.

There was, for example, an officer observed during this project who was reported by other officers to be unduly aggressive and rude as he did his job. They indicated that he liked to "jack people up" and "get in their faces." By making them angry with him, he obtained an excuse for using force against them. Indeed, this officer was observed repeatedly insulting, challenging, and threatening citizens in a manner that seemed disproportional to their behavior. He even verbally challenged witnesses and onlookers as they watched unfolding events. (The officer *was not* observed to actually use force in any of these cases.) Such behaviors, importantly, did detract from the officer's ability to achieve his, the department's, and the community's goals. Subjects of investigation regularly challenged his authority, witnesses were reluctant to provide him with information, and his supervisors complained that such factors caused him to take a lot longer to resolve cases than other officers required. In failing to match an effective strategy to the real requirements of the situation at hand, then, the officer's work can be understood as a failure.

Moreover, his fellow officers were critical of the officer's work on the grounds that it caused them problems as well. More than one officer noted that citizens do not see police as individuals;

rather, "all they see is the uniform." They complained that when the officer behaved aggressively and rudely, his behavior "rubbed off," making citizens less willing to support them and help them do their jobs. Thus, the officers themselves assumed that their actions had the kind of socially significant role that has been argued throughout this book and were critical of a fellow officer whose actions harmed their ability to do their jobs effectively. In other words, they wanted the officer to act as a leader so they could as well.

A third type of failure can occur if workers do not choose to pursue legitimate objectives or outcomes in varying situations. That is, while workers may have to exercise discretion in deciding what should be done in a specific case, they might choose badly or base their decisions on illegitimate standards. Representative examples might include a police officer who more readily stops vehicles driven by minorities or social-service workers who remove children only from homes that are poor.

At least two stories discussed in the Preface can be interpreted as this type of failure. One case involved the arrest of a woman who had passed out in her car. As was discussed in the Preface, the woman had been involved in a widely publicized family tragedy a week before her arrest. As a consequence, two of the three officers at the scene argued that the woman should not have been arrested. They thought that she should have been driven to her nearby home and allowed to deal with her trauma in private, that her drunkenness was understandable under the circumstances, and that she did not pose a danger to the general community. Further, in subsequent conversation with the observer, they claimed that the arrest only occurred because the DWI/DUI task force officer was trying to "bump his stats." In essence, they argued that the third officer was not acting as a leader, that he was not properly considering the broader context of his decisions and was only narrowly following his job description. Such actions, they thought, were illegitimate, and they were upset that the department's rules gave the third officer precedence in this case.

Another case discussed in the Preface also illustrates the failure to act as a transformational leader. The case in which a social-service worker did not fully investigate or respond to the needs and condition of an elderly woman can be seen as a situation in which a worker failed to think about what could be done in a creative or effective way. Instead, she viewed her role as a narrowly bureaucratic one: she answered the call, established that minimum conditions existed, and left. As a consequence, an elderly, apparently mentally challenged, if not incompetent, woman was left to fend for herself without adequate food or electricity. Given that such assistance was available and fairly readily provided, the worker's choice can be seen as a failure to think creatively about how best to fulfill the client's needs, the department's role, and society's good.

The final category of leadership failures, "uncertain," encompasses those cases in which leaders take what are understood by local standards to be legitimate and effective steps to establish and accomplish goals, but these standards may be questioned over time. Police officers enforcing segregation laws were supported by the majority of white citizens in most of the South, for example, but regardless of this "local" legitimacy, their actions were morally questionable. The reality that local standards may be illegitimate within a broader context needs to be admitted, and as a consequence, so does the possibility that workers acting in such environments are failing to act as leaders in the largest sense of the term.

Perhaps the most clear example of uncertainty in terms of worker leadership involved a vehicle pursuit conducted by a group of police officers one night. In the midst of an extremely slow shift, one in which the radio remained silent for over an hour at a time, a number of officers assembled at a central location to talk, relax, and generally pass the time. Suddenly, a bright red Ford Mustang ran the traffic light near the location where the officers were assembled. As he crossed the intersection, the driver saw the police cars and punched the accelerator, peeling through the intersection and attempting to escape the expected pursuit.

The change that went through the assembled officers was electric. Each rushed to his car to pursue the Mustang. There was, formally, no real decision making going on; the officers saw a violator, saw him try to escape, and scrambled to respond. Once the officers caught up with the speeding vehicle, they adopted a standard pursuit protocol: one officer led the pursuit; a second, trailing vehicle handled the radio traffic related to the chase; and other officers spread throughout the area to try to cut off any escape routes. They then followed the vehicle, closely but not too closely, as it ran down residential streets at a high rate of speed.

As the pursuit proceeded, the officer leading the chase, with whom the observer was riding, decided to slow and not follow the Mustang at its excessive rate of speed. He explained, while slowing, that it wasn't worth causing an accident to catch a traffic offender. However, just as he was finishing his explanation, he came upon a crash scene. The Mustang had failed to negotiate a turn, crossed four lanes of roadway, and crashed into a large tree. The driver, who was not seriously injured, was ticketed and arrested. His two passengers, both of whom were slightly injured, were released.

In one sense, this case can be seen as a success. Traffic laws are important. Every year, traffic accidents kill thousands of people. The community has an interest in being protected from vehicles traveling at excessive rates of speed. Officers are empowered to arrest suspects who violate such laws and are trained to drive effectively in such cases. Both the law and departmental procedures gave officers the right to undertake such actions. And the officer's decision to back off of the chase was clearly effective: the situation's danger was demonstrated by the suspect's subsequent accident.

Yet, more broadly, communities around the United States are beginning to question police pursuit policies. Despite the very real adrenaline "rush" that accompanies such chases, and despite the public relations image of police officers tracking down "bad guys" that such events embody, there are very real risks involved during police pursuits. Police, suspects, and innocent bystanders have been seriously hurt and even killed during such pursuits, despite the fact that the crime that starts the pursuit is often only a misdemeanor (i.e., speeding, running a stop sign, etc.).

Thus, while it is absolutely the case that the pursuit described here was legal, within department guidelines, and effective, it is reasonable to question the pursuit as such. The original offense was running a red light; a call could have gone out to patrolling officers to look for the red Mustang and stop it if they found it. If the driver was not being pursued by a large group of officers, whose presence seemed to stimulate the escape attempt in the first place, he might have voluntarily stopped if he had been found. Instead, several people got hurt, many vehicles were endangered as they stood parked on the side of the road, police officers and other drivers were put at risk, and somebody went to jail. While this case was not strictly a failure, leadership theory provides a means by which the appropriateness and legitimacy of the officers' actions can be questioned or confirmed in a broader context.

CONCLUSION

It is clear, then, that street-level workers can act as leaders as they do their jobs. Like leaders, they balance values, ideals, norms, and principles in deciding what to do and establish the legitimacy of their decisions within this context. Moreover, they employ a range of options, strategies, and techniques in support of these goals, depending on situational factors. If they misuse or abuse the discretion they are given, they are not acting as leaders. Viewed as leaders, however, the factors that shape their work can be illustrated, the relative legitimacy of their actions can be established, and the importance of their work can be demonstrated.

5

Conclusions and Implications

The Work of Street-Level Public Servants: The Case of the Irresponsible Fourth Grader

A call came to child protective services from the police department that an officer had picked up a nine-year-old child who had apparently been abandoned by his mother in the downtown area of the city. The police had a report of one prior arrest on the mother for drunk driving. The social-services agency had dealt with the woman in the past when she had packed the bags of the child's older brother, set them on the porch, and told him to leave when he was twelve years old. The records also indicated that she was an alcoholic.

On her way to meet the police officer and pick up the boy, the worker told the observer that her tentative plan was to go to the boy's house and give the mother a legal notice that the department would be taking temporary custody of the child. She would then place the boy with a relative (probably his adult brother) or in foster care until the investigation could be completed. She explained, however, that she was only talking about a tentative plan. "We'll have to see what's going on."

When she arrived at the meeting place, the boy was sitting in the back of the police car, apparently talking with the officer and another child of about the same age standing outside the police car. It was about 8 p.m. and growing dark. He appeared unharmed but tired. The officer got out of the car and told the worker that the mother had abandoned him downtown in an unfamiliar neighborhood at about 3 p.m.

that afternoon. The boy had wandered around for some time and then gone into a veterinarian's office and told them he was lost. The receptionist had called the police.

The worker then walked back to the car with the police officer and talked briefly with the boy. She asked if he was okay and some general questions about what happened to him when he got in trouble. The boy said he did not know and slumped down in the seat of the car.

The worker walked back to her car to check the address and to see that she had the proper paperwork. The officer followed her and asked what she was going to do. "You aren't taking him back home are you?" he said. She told him that she didn't know. He looked at her with a mixture of disbelief and disgust. She explained that, by law, she needed to make a reasonable effort to find the parents in the case of abandonment. She thanked him for his help. The officer shook his head and walked away.

The boy then got in the worker's car and they drove to the mother's apartment. The worker knocked on the door and the mother answered. When she saw her son she made no comment, just watched him walk in. The boy showed no fear of his mother, but not much interest either. The mother appeared to be angry, but not enraged. She was clean, neat, and appeared to be sober. She asked no questions and made no comments. She looked expectantly at the worker.

The worker asked if she could come into the apartment. The mother said, "Yes, I don't want to talk to you people out here. I don't like people knowing my business." The apartment itself was immaculate—everything was extremely neat, clean, and orderly. There were numerous knickknacks, artificial flowers, figurines, and other decorations, all precisely arranged, layered, and displayed.

After asking if she could sit down, the worker asked if she could speak to the mother privately. The mother refused, saying that she had no secrets from her son and then telling him to stay in the room. The worker then asked the mother, "Can you tell me what happened today?" The mother said, "It was just stress," and fell silent. The worker asked again about what happened. The mother responded, "It's his own fault. I'm trying to teach him what he needs to know. I'm trying to teach him to clean. He doesn't learn." She gestured toward a table with an elaborate display of flowers, purses, gloves, and other objects and said, "He won't put things back the way they were." She continued, "We were at the store today and I bought cigarettes. He wasn't watching and we lost them. It gets old after a while. It's a lot of money to lose." She looked at her son. "I told him, you are never there for me. It's supposed to be a team effort." Shaking her head, she added, "I try to teach him. He needs to drink the knowledge."

After talking for a moment longer, the worker asked the mother if she was okay and if she was taking any medication. The mother said that she was supposed to be taking Elavil, Prozac, and Klonopin, but that she had only been taking the Prozac. The worker asked if she was getting mental health services. The mother said she was. The worker asked if the mother had been to counseling with her son. She said that she had. The worker asked for information so that she could verify the mother's claim.

The mother said, "He wants me to nurture him so much. I need nurturing too." The worker asked, "Were you worried about him today?" She responded, "Even when you're down and out, you don't talk to strangers. I was worried about that." She paused, looked down, and said quietly, "I told him I didn't want him anymore."

In a calm voice, the worker said, "It seems like you are very stressed. Do you understand why we are here?" The worker paused, and continued, "Your son was abandoned and the police may be filing a child-neglect charge against you. I have to make sure your son is safe. Tell me what you could have done differently today." The mother responded in a tired voice, "If he doesn't watch his stuff, someone will steal it from him—his girlfriend or wife. He needs to learn." She shook her head and said, "I always have to know everything and be everything. I get tired. It was a scare tactic. I had to show him."

The worker said, "You are stressed. You have a lot to be stressed about. But you are the adult. Leaving him on the street is <u>not</u> okay." The mother nodded, "I left him a long way away, too."

The worker asked to see the boy's room and to check the kitchen to make sure there was adequate food. The boy's room was clean and neat. Along with a television and a video game, there were posters on the wall, mostly of women in skimpy bathing suits. The kitchen was well-stocked with food. As she walked back into the living room, the mother said, "He's my whole life. We laugh and play. We ride bikes. I am everything to him. I just get tired."

The worker asked the mother if she felt like she was going to hurt herself or her son. "No," she said, shaking her head vigorously. The worker asked if she would abandon her son again. The mother responded, "I don't know. He has to learn. He has to drink knowledge."

The worker then suggested to the mother that all parents need to get some time away from their children on occasion. She told the mother about after-school care and other alternative care arrangements. She also offered to help make arrangements for her son to stay with relatives for a couple of days. The mother refused, saying her son needed to stay with her.

The worker went to the back room and called her supervisor. She explained that the mother was not willing to voluntarily place the child with a relative. The supervisor then asked if she felt that the child was in imminent danger. The worker said that while he was probably not in immediate danger, he might be in danger over the long term. Together they made a decision to open a case for ongoing monitoring, but not to take the child out of the home that night.

The worker visited the home every day for the next several days and checked to make sure that follow-up services were being provided. She told the observer later, "I am still really uncomfortable. But I cannot prove that she is abusing him. Emotional abuse is the hardest to prove in court." She also noted that, under the circumstances, the suggestive posters in his room bothered her. She said, "He's only a fourth grader, but his mother obviously wants him to be her partner and to take care of her. I will put it all in my notes, but if I can't prove it, we can't take him out of there. At this point, the best we can do is to try to help them. But I don't like it. I just don't like it."

INTRODUCTION

This book has argued for a new model of street-level public service based on the concept of leadership. This argument has been built on an examination of three concepts: discretion, power, and legitimacy, as applied to the experience of real street-level workers dealing with the challenges of public service. We began with the idea that street-level public employees regularly exercise significant amounts of discretion as they do their jobs. This discretion is inevitable, given the complex situations and problems these workers confront, the conflictual environment in which they work, and the fact that they must operate largely independent of direct supervision. Workers must interpret and balance a welter of competing and sometimes conflicting norms, rules, expectations, laws, and values while making decisions on the street. Moreover, we suggested that the scope and nature of this street-level discretion has expanded because of changes in citizen expectations, management systems, and political climate, and the increasingly "wicked" nature of the problems these workers confront.

We asserted that although existing models of public service provide important insights, they do not realistically portray the contemporary challenges of street-level public service. In particular, they fail to provide a framework for fully addressing the problem of worker accountability. Discretion, in order to be exercised appropriately, must be legitimated by some set of standards. Thus, we suggested that discretionary acts, rather than being good because they are necessary, are good only in relation to a balance of values and ideals as they relate to a specific set of circumstances.

We then argued that the tension between discretion and accountability is particularly significant for street-level public servants. There are many different perspectives from which their work can be evaluated. The norms and expectations of their agencies, communities, clients, and their own individual values often crosscut and sometimes present unresolvable differences. Thus, the question was posed, "How can the actions of street-level public servants be legitimated?"

We concluded that the concept of leadership is a useful and appropriate framework for considering questions of legitimacy and discretion in front-line public service. Based on hundreds of hours of observation, the street-level leadership model was found to be descriptively accurate in terms of the choice-making responsibilities of workers such as police officers and social-service workers. From a normative standpoint, the model was shown to provide a framework for the development of standards against which the performance of these workers can be judged. Rather than an all-or-nothing theory of legitimacy in public service, the concept of leadership provides a means by which standards of accountability can be derived for specific actions in specific situations. And, importantly, such standards and behaviors were demonstrated in the work of street-level public servants. Such workers are, or at least can be, leaders as they do their jobs, and the legitimacy of their actions can be evaluated through standards expressed in the concept of leadership.

This chapter revisits the question of why a change in how we think or theorize about street-level public service is important. It then explores the implications of the street-level leadership model for workers, their agencies, and the governance system. It concludes with some ideas about how street-level leadership can be fostered and supported by workers, public organizations, citizens, and policy makers.

THE POWER OF THEORIZING

As noted in the introduction to Chapter One, this book has proceeded from the premise that theory and language exert a powerful influence over how workers define themselves and their responsibilities; how agencies recruit, train, and manage these employees; and ultimately, how we define the role these workers play in the governance process. So, while a key focus of this book has been to describe the day-to-day challenges and realities of being a frontline public servant, an underlying purpose has been to suggest a different way of thinking about the roles and responsibilities of these workers in a broader sense.

Theory and practice are often contrasted, in that the latter is seen as meaningful in the "practical world" and the former is viewed as being of interest only to scholars. A different perspective on theory and practice is suggested here. As Kaplan expressed it,

> Theory is of practice, and must stand or fall with its practicality . . . a theory is a way of making sense out of a disturbing situation so as to allow us most effectively to bring to bear our

repertoire of habits, and even more important, to modify habits or discard them altogether. . . . [So] theorizing may be a very practical activity indeed (n.d., 295–296).

Kirlin and Thompson were expressing the same sort of idea when they said that "Theory provides understanding of the meaning of what is going on and of possible causes . . . [and] strategies for action" (1987, 77). Theory then, provides a framework for understanding and explaining a situation in a manner which enables and informs action.

Viewed from this perspective, one of the most potent and effective ways to influence practice is to change the theory and language used to understand that practice. Accordingly, we argue that the street-level leadership model can play a vital role in helping citizens, communities, legislators, clients, agencies, and workers themselves struggle with the problems and issues that they encounter in frontline public service. In fact, in the long run, changing how we think about street-level public service may be much more important and valuable than the sorts of incremental, stand alone organizational reforms (such as the introduction of new management controls, performance measurement systems, and so on) that are more commonly recommended.

The language used to express theory is critical. The language chosen "affects not only our understanding of theories, but also our perceptions of, and preferences for, theories" (Kirlin and Thompson 1987, 77). The language chosen is important in part because theories gain acceptance through dialogue. In dialogue that is carried out in Congress and state legislatures, city councils, and courtrooms, in newspapers and journals, on the street and in private living rooms, in novels, and on television, differing views and theoretical perspectives about government employees are both implicitly and explicitly espoused. Not only are differing theoretical perspectives on the role of public employees in governance debated, but so are alternative theories on the characteristics and capacities of public servants themselves. The outcome of this debate, in a very real sense, constrains or enables action by these individuals and institutions.

For example, in the Volcker Commission Report, the "erosion in the quality of the public service" was said to have *resulted* from a lack of public trust and a widespread belief that the government lacks efficacy (1989, 2). If this is so, put in the terminology of theory, the most widely shared contemporary theory with regard to public service must be that it is inefficient and ineffectual. In some ways, it does not really matter whether the theory was initially drawn from observed experience or whether the theory came first. In either case, it is still apparent that the explanation or theory itself became self-fulfilling, or truer to experience, as the theory gained acceptance. Put simply, to the extent that the public believes that public servants cannot and will not act effectively, thoughtfully, and responsibly, it makes it much more difficult for public servants to do so and much less likely that their actions will be interpreted and judged as being so.

From this perspective, it is not an overstatement to suggest that the capacity of the governance system and the efficacy of public administration as a component of that system are products of the acceptance of a particular set of theories which undergird them. Accordingly, the language used to characterize public servants facilitates or constrains action within the field. In short, theory is that which makes the practice of public administration possible or impossible, as the case may be. As a result, theoretical changes such as those suggested here have important implications for individual workers, for public organizations, and for the larger system of governance.

IMPLICATIONS OF THE STREET-LEVEL LEADERSHIP MODEL

What are the implications of using the theoretical lens of the street-level leadership model to understand the roles and responsibilities of street-level public servants and to assess the legitimacy of their discretionary choices? What difference does the model make to workers, to public agencies, and to society as a whole? The following sections explore these questions and then consider how street-level leadership can be encouraged, shaped, and effectively implemented on the street so that workers can use discretion creatively and legitimately to achieve public objectives.

Street-Level Leadership and the Worker

From a relatively simplistic point of view, it can be argued that to the extent that the model describes what street-level public servants are already doing and embodies standards by which they already evaluate their work, the consequences for the actual work performed may be negligible. But the real import of the model is not in changing the work that is performed, but in changing the way that workers think about and define themselves and their jobs.

The workers in this study were well aware of the challenges and complexities inherent in their work. They were also aware of the competing roles, expectations, rules, values, and norms that influenced what they did and how they did it. They often said things like, "I know my title is investigator, but that is not what I spend most of my time doing," or "I am a police officer, but I spend more time talking to people than chasing bad guys." They were able to conceptualize how differing situations called for differing responses and how their behavior and decisions were dictated by the circumstances they confronted. They knew that the decisions they were making were very important ones and that they often involved difficult value conflicts. What they lacked was the language to describe how they coped with it.

Workers were also acutely aware of the power they exercised in balancing these values when making decisions. For example, in discussing a case, one worker commented, "Cases like this remind me of how much power I have. It's scary." Another said, "I go home at night and I think, *I* made these decisions." Finally, one worker summed it up by saying simply, "You have power. You have to know how to use it."

Although workers may have known implicitly that they were behaving as leaders as they did their jobs, they did not use the word. In some cases, after the observations, workers asked the researchers questions about what the study had found. In response, they were told about the concept of street-level leadership. Invariably, they expressed agreement that street-level leadership is what they do. Many also seemed gratified and pleased to have a way to talk about and understand the demands that they face. But these workers also frequently commented on the fact that others did not see it the same way.

So what would the acceptance of the street-level leadership model do for individual workers? While it is difficult to say with certainty what the effects on individual workers would be, some probable implications for most workers can be suggested. First, it would help workers to conceptualize and articulate what their jobs are in a realistically complex manner. In other words, it would give them a way to describe their work that matches their own conceptions of it. While workers are aware of the challenges and demands that they face, most have no systematic framework within which they can consider and articulate how they balance competing pressures, information, and rules to make choices. Leadership, as a concept, explicitly directs their attention to precisely the kinds of issues of value conflict and dissent that characterize much of what they do. Using such terms to understand and shape their choices can be expected to give workers the tools they need to more fully and effectively do their jobs.

Second, the model of street-level leadership can be empowering to frontline workers, many of whom struggle with the negative stereotypes of public service. The term "leadership" is an inherently positive one. Instead of being "bureaucrats" who take people's children away or give traffic tickets when they should be out catching bad guys, the term "leader" is more consistent with the societal importance of the work they do. Using the language of leadership may provide a measure of pride and reinforcement that is badly needed among frontline public servants. There are many workers who believe, maybe rightly so, that the public does not appreciate or understand the demanding, exhausting, and important work they perform. Worse, many believe that the public hates them. These workers, who devote their lives to serving the public, need symbols and words that help to counteract this hostility and, maybe more importantly, to change it.

Third, by providing workers with a language with which to articulate and respond to the many competing expectations that shape their actions, the model also can be expected to enhance workers' sense of competence. That is, when confronted by an often-endless string of negative, painful conflicts, workers may understand that they have the creative potential to shape events in new and valuable ways. Leaders can draw on explicit and latent values as they do their work. To the degree that agencies, clients, and communities support the choices they make in light of these values conflicts, workers can be expected to feel more capable of influencing, if not resolving, varied cases.

Fourth, the street-level leadership model can help to highlight for workers not only the importance of what they do, but also the responsibilities and accountabilities that go along with the discretion they must exercise. The model recognizes both the significance of their work and the power of their choices. As such, it helps workers to remain cognizant of the larger implications of their choices for their peers, their supervisors, their agency, their communities, and the larger system of governance.

Further, the street-level leadership model can help workers to understand the continuum of effectiveness and ineffectiveness that they must navigate, given the competing expectations, fluid circumstances, and conflicting rules and norms that they face. Workers are confronted with situations and problems that cannot be resolved in a manner that satisfies all values, norms, and rules, and at the same time have a positive outcome for both the client and the community. However, as was argued in Chapter Three, leaders face such situations all the time. Leadership is not judged on the basis of whether or not everyone is happy. Rather, questions of motivation, goal orientation, the appropriateness of the leader's behaviors and choices, and the results that are achieved are the means through which leadership is evaluated. Thus, the street-level leadership model provides a framework from which workers can assess their own relative effectiveness on the basis of circumstances they confront and the goals they attempt to achieve. This is critically important to workers who may feel defeated by the sometimes-intractable, even insurmountable, problems they must confront on a daily basis.

Finally, viewing street-level public servants as leaders promotes recognition of the interconnectedness of such workers with other dimensions of the governance system. Leaders work in environments of followers, laws, rules, norms, and so on. They have tools and skills with which they can work to achieve their goals, but, without the support of others in the system, their efforts will ultimately be unsuccessful and ineffective. Workers, then, need not feel that they are patrolling the streets or investigating incidents with the expectation that they alone are to solve the problems at hand. Rather, they are one part of a larger system. While they have unique and powerful opportunities to shape what that system does, they are still just a part of the whole. Thus, their failures and successes are, to some degree, shared enterprises; workers need not feel that the whole burden of society is on their shoulders.

Accordingly, to the extent that communities, agencies, clients, and workers themselves begin to redefine frontline public servants as street-level leaders, they may begin to appreciate the difficult jobs that these individuals perform and provide the support and assistance that these workers need in order to accomplish public objectives. While such a change may be difficult to achieve, any movement in this direction will not only improve the work life of these individuals, but can also be expected to improve the quality of life in communities across the country as it enables street-level public servants to do their jobs better.

Street-Level Leadership and Public Organizations

The street-level leadership model also has a number of important implications for public organizations, supervisors, and administrators. First, to the degree that the model promotes the creativity, empowerment, and capabilities of workers, it may help agencies to fulfill their missions better. Engaged, thoughtful workers who understand the value of their work are far more likely to do their difficult jobs successfully and effectively. Moreover, workers who understand and can articulate how the legitimacy of their choices can be assessed and established are likely to feel more empowered and effective than those who live in fear of reproach and condemnation. That is, police officers, social-service workers, and other public servants who act as leaders can be expected to be more effective in achieving their goals. To the extent that this expectation is realized, agencies will also benefit.

Second, the street-level leadership model provides agencies with a new way of thinking about the roles and responsibilities of their workers in framing communications with citizens and elected officials. As was the case with workers themselves, viewing public servants as leaders gives agencies a different perspective from which to view and account for their employees' actions and choices. This shift in thinking provides a framework for agencies to consider multiple factors, values, and pressures that influence their workers. Doing so can change how they justify to citizens and policy makers what their workers do and why they do it, and why investments to support and enhance their effectiveness are warranted. In the process of educating legislators, citizens, the media, and clients about the agency's role and mission and the role front-line workers play in achieving that mission, leadership is a powerful descriptive and evaluative tool.

Third, if street-level leaders are in fact more effective and successful in dealing with situations on the street, this will help departments to build better community and media relations. Skilled street-level leaders not only handle problems better, but positively influence others in advancing shared goals. As such, street-level leaders play an important role in shaping the public image of a department. Effective street-level leadership will not only enhance public relations; public support, in turn, can enhance the ability of workers to meet community objectives.

Additionally, supervisors and administrators, by using the language of leadership, can begin to communicate to workers the importance of their work while emphasizing the importance of accountability. Positive messages about the value of what these people do for their agencies and communities are critically important. The language of street-level leadership is a powerful tool to help reinforce the role that agencies and communities need these workers to play in responding to complex and extraordinarily difficult societal problems. It also opens the door for supervisors and workers to talk about the importance of their choices in the larger context. Doing so can improve the quality of supervisory relationships to the benefit of workers, supervisors, and the organization.

Cumulatively, then, viewing public servants as street-level leaders can be expected to provide a number of advantages to agencies. In changing the terms in which communities, clients, and legislators interpret and evaluate the agency and its workers, and by enhancing the effectiveness of employees, the concept has real, positive implications for public organizations.

Street-Level Leadership and Governance

Perhaps the most important implications of the street-level leadership model are for the governance system. After all, the most pressing and important dilemmas facing American society are not organizational problems; they are governance problems in the most fundamental sense. The governance system is beset with problems of paralysis, public mistrust, and "wicked" public policy issues. As stated in the Volcker Commission Report, *Leadership for America*, the country now confronts "a world of enormous complexity and awesome risks . . . we are assaulted daily by new social, environmental, and health issues almost incomprehensible in scope and impact" (1989, 2).

The ability of American society to meet these challenges is largely dependent on the vitality and capacity of the governance system, and on the public service as a critical component of that system. How can frontline public service be most appropriately used to advance sound and effective democratic governance? Problems of governance cannot be addressed by closely curtailing discretion exercised by frontline public employees. Such an approach ignores the realities of the street. Simply giving street-level workers freedom to do what they think is right or appropriate is not the answer, either. This approach ignores the bureaucratic and legal environment in which these workers operate.

Street-level workers play a role in governance that is both bureaucratic *and* political, characterized by high levels of discretion exercised within a broad and complex system of accountability. As Dwight Waldo asserted, "The simple-minded notion that the governmental realm can be clearly divided between the political and the administrative is uninformed and untrue." He also suggested, however, that "the doctrine was not all wrong" (1981, 82). There are sound reasons for this dualism. Perhaps the best justification for this seeming contradiction is that an acceptance of both the validity and the limitations of a distinction between politics and administration, between discretion and accountability, between the choices of the individual worker and the need for legitimacy, best captures the reality of practice. The characterization used by Edley in his analysis of administrative decision making is apt: "Sound governmental decision making . . . require[s] a combination of . . . paradigms" (1990, 222). He likened the integration of the political, scientific, and adjudicatory fairness paradigms of decision making to the yin and yang of classical Chinese cosmology, which "are separately describable yet always combined in nature" (1990, 223).

Accordingly, the notion of street-level leadership may be best understood as presenting an integration in action of seemingly inconsistent theories and models. On one hand, street-level leaders are bureaucrats in that they work for bureaucratic organizations and their actions are constrained by them. But they are also policy makers, implementers, power wielders, professionals, problem solvers, and political actors. The key, however, is that they play all of these roles within a system of accountability that is, and ought to be, complex and demanding. If the exercise of discretion by frontline bureaucrats is understood as leadership, workers are not "problems" who distort the application of policies through their abuse of discretion. Nor are they autonomous actors whose actions should not be questioned. Rather, they are active, accountable, and responsible participants in governance who play different roles under different circumstances.

When viewed as leaders, these workers can be seen to work within a complex matrix of values, rules, expectations, and goals that shape their behaviors and form the standards by which their performance ought to be judged. These standards are, in part, based on the values and preferences of the community at large. While citizens may not always agree with the choices made, the broader terms of this disagreement can be discussed constructively within the leadership model. Street-level workers, then, are not outsiders who impose a bureaucracy's abstract ideals on some community. Rather, they are members of that community who play an important role in governance by balancing community values, legal and organizational constraints, and a variety of other factors in a manner that can be legitimated relative to a particular situation.

What such workers do, then, is an extension of the community, not an abstraction of it. This further suggests that what workers do may be more accessible to members of the community through the model of street-level leadership. That is, when the work that street-level public servants do is interpreted as leadership, it provides citizens with a different and more immediate way to evaluate the decisions workers make and the actions they take. Rather than imposing "standard operating procedures" that most citizens have probably had little influence in shaping, street-level leaders make choices to achieve goals in particular contexts. Street-level leaders can and should be responsive to community values and citizen concerns. Consequently, citizens can consider and interpret their work in very different terms than is currently the case.

Finally, talking about workers as street-level leaders can encourage citizens to have higher expectations for public-service workers. This is potentially important for a number of reasons. First, people who expect good things from frontline public servants can be expected to actively engage with and support those workers. Thus, rather than resisting or avoiding workers when they enter communities, citizens dealing with street-level leaders may approach those workers, provide them with needed information and perspectives, and establish continuing relationships. Such relationships, which are already emphasized in some community

policing and child-outreach programs, have already been demonstrated to be effective in improving delivery of public services and
accomplishing public objectives.

Conversely, it may also be the case that some workers live
down to the expectations citizens have of them. Low public expectations of workers can encourage them to invest very little time
and energy in their work—which is, after all, often depressing,
overwhelming, and intractable. By contrast, when communities
expect the best and give workers the tools to achieve these expectations, good things can be expected to occur. Street-level leadership provides citizens with a means by which to encourage workers
to do their best and help to achieve society's goals.

Taken together, the concept of street-level leadership provides
a lens through which to view workers as creative, effective participants in the governance system. It promotes the notion of
accountable discretion in terms that are accessible to policy makers, legislators, communities, clients, citizens, and workers themselves. Finally, it empowers workers and suggests a means by which
they can more effectively and legitimately achieve the important
tasks to which they are dedicated.

CREATING STREET-LEVEL LEADERSHIP

The street-level leadership model has a number of significant and
positive advantages for workers, for agencies, and for the governance system. In order to realize these advantages, a number of
changes are needed to help create and enhance street-level leadership. Specifically, there are a number of things that workers, agencies, and policy makers can do to support street-level leadership in
the public service.

Changing Workers

At the most fundamental level, implementing street-level leadership is about shaping the way frontline workers think about and
do their jobs. Street-level leadership requires workers who are
motivated, engaged, and sensitive to the values conflicts that they
confront. The first and perhaps most significant step in that direction is for workers to redefine their self-images and expectations.
Rather than simply carrying out the narrow dictates of a specific

agency, street-level leaders need to think of themselves as operating in the context of a wide range of pressures, norms, and expectations as they do their jobs. Leadership is an active, creative process in which leaders have to engage with the issues and difficulties in the circumstances at hand. This requires workers to be aware of and responsive to the rules established by their agencies, the ultimate goals of authorizing legislation, and the broader values of the community at large. This is a fundamentally different view of their roles than is commonly understood to be the case.

Workers will need to make the decision to accept and embrace broader responsibilities than they are formally charged with at present. Generally, workers indicated that they were required to follow departmental procedures in activities like, for police, raiding a building or searching a car, or, for social-service workers, contacting certain individuals when investigating a child-abuse claim. Most importantly, they explained, they were expected to fill out their paperwork properly and on time. But while such matters are important, they do not encompass the real jobs that these workers perform and certainly do not capture the essence of leadership. Workers know this, but there is generally little recognition of this fact evident in their official duties and responsibilities. Workers need to explicitly accept that their jobs entail much broader responsibilities for dealing with people, making decisions, and weighing variables, and that they should be held accountable for their performance in these areas. While agencies and policy makers certainly play a central role in making this happen, ultimately it is the workers who must accept the responsibility.

Although changes at the organizational level are critical, there are still things that frontline workers can do on their own to practice street-level leadership. In handling and responding to issues and problems, workers can begin by asking themselves questions such as:

- What kinds of choices does this situation demand? Am I making choices about what to do, how to do it, or both?
- If I need to decide *what to do*, what are the factors that I need to consider? What does the law say? Departmental policy? What are the needs of the "clients" (however defined)? Are there other people present that I need to consider? What does my supervisor want? What if my decisions appear in

the newspaper tomorrow? How do my more experienced
coworkers respond? Do other agencies play a role? What do
I think is right? What are the conflicts between these factors
and how am I going to balance those conflicts? Is there a
higher value that can be advanced by doing so?

- If I know what needs to be done, but I need to decide *how to
  do it*, what are the key characteristics of the situation? Are
  the clients cooperative or not? Are there others present who
  can help me? What are the departmental rules and laws
  which govern my actions? What is the least amount of coercion that I can use to reach the goal? Am I varying my
  response as the situation unfolds? Am I supporting people in
  making appropriate choices and directing them when they
  are not?

While it may be suggested that such questions are onerous and
unrealistically complicated, our observations indicate that the
opposite is true. These are precisely the types of questions that
effective street-level public servants ask themselves already. In one
sense, all the street-level leadership model does is affirm and make
explicit the complex discretionary choices that these workers face
on a daily basis. As noted in the previous chapter, the street-level
leadership model is best thought of as representing a style of
thinking rather than as dictating a cumbersome decision-making
procedure. By adopting this style of thinking or perspective, workers can use the concept of leadership to make more effective
choices and to consider and explain the legitimacy of their discretionary decisions.

Changing Organizations

While individual workers can do a great deal to advance the
notion of street-level leadership, there are also important steps that
public organizations can take to more effectively develop and
encourage workers to act as leaders. Some of the changes that will
be required at the organizational level derive from the changes
that need to occur within the workers themselves. As workers redefine their roles and responsibilities, managers and organizational
executives will also need to reorient their understanding of workers. Line-level public servants, rather than just being employees,
are also leaders and have to be considered as such. Workers need to

be treated as responsible choice makers, not implementers of policy.

This reconceptualization has several important implications. First, organizations must carefully consider the types of individuals who are recruited and selected to do these jobs. The work that they perform demands strong communication skills, the flexibility to adapt to changing circumstances, the ability to understand and articulate competing values, sound judgment, and intelligence— skills and abilities needed by all leaders (Gardner 1990; Yukl 1994). Similarly, the ability to conceptualize and articulate issues related to competing roles, values, and norms seems particularly important. Although education was not a factor directly dealt with in the study, the relationship between conceptual abilities and education may be an issue for further research. To the extent that higher education helps individuals to develop conceptual reasoning, tolerance for ambiguity, and the ability to articulate clearly, one may expect those with higher education levels also to be more effective street-level leaders. Accordingly, agencies may need to rethink job standards that do not require a college degree.

Second, street-level leaders require a very different kind of training than that which the workers observed for this study indicated they had received. Most workers said that they were trained in procedures and paperwork, but were not given training that prepared them for the full range of responsibilities and choices that they had to make. There are many leadership training programs that can be tailored to help teach the kinds of skills and values necessary in carrying out street-level leadership responsibilities. Such training should focus on the inculcation of values and the articulation and attainment of goals. If workers can be trained to recognize the core values that underlie a particular program, especially if they recognize that these values have ties to the interests and expectations of both the organization and the community at large, then the employee's actions can be shaped in ways that will support the goals of the program. It is also important to provide training to help street-level leaders become more adept at diagnosing the characteristics of situations and altering their behaviors to achieve desired outcomes more effectively.

Admittedly, some important leadership skills are difficult to acquire through formal training programs. For example, conceptual and interpersonal skills are difficult to teach directly. However, case studies, simulations, videotapes, and role playing can be used effectively, particularly if they provide opportunities to observe, practice, and receive feedback on what approaches are more and less effective (Yukl 1994).

While training workers in "core" leadership skills is important, agencies may also need to think realistically about other skill areas that workers need in managing the complex mix of tasks their jobs require. For example, workers may benefit from training in crisis counseling, first aid, conflict management, pharmacology, ethics, and other areas. In other words, while agencies may have an interest in defining a worker's primary role rather narrowly (patrol officer, case worker, or investigator, for example) these workers also need preparation for their broader and often more complex roles in interacting with the public.

Although formal training is unquestionably important, opportunities to learn from experience are also critical. As Gardner puts it, most "leadership development is done within the context of its normal, day to day work supervision" (1990, 173). He points out that it is critical that supervisors not "squelch" leaders. In the context of street-level leaders, it is important to acknowledge that the problems they face are complex and that the judgments they make may be different than the judgments a supervisor would make if he or she was in the field. Workers must be given opportunities to make choices with the expectation that they will need to be able to articulate and justify why they did what they did. They also need to know that if they do, they will be supported by their supervisors and agency management.

Experiential learning is also enhanced by modeling, coaching, and mentoring. Workers learn desired values and behaviors from positive role models, whether they be supervisors or peers. Agencies can facilitate this process by teaming experienced, effective frontline workers with less experienced ones. Agencies can also work to create expectations that supervisors will work to model and inculcate leadership values such as responsibility, accountability, and judgment in the face of competing cross-pressures and difficult choices. Supervisors can, when possible, engage employees in discussions of difficult situations and problems encountered by other workers in order to allow all workers to learn from mistakes. In a sense, this creates real-time case studies of more and less effective street-level leadership in action.

Viewing public servants as street-level leaders also has implications for how workers' performance is evaluated. Measures of productivity, adherence to rules, and accomplishment of discrete tasks, while important, may be inadequate to foster the development of street-level leadership. Leaders, as was discussed previously, can be evaluated best through the goals toward which they act and the appropriateness of the steps they take to achieve these goals. Evaluating workers under old procedural standards while expecting them to meet new demands for successful and effective results is virtually guaranteed to produce failure. Employee performance can be evaluated in terms of questions like: Did the employee's decisions and actions support the program's purposes? Did the employee act appropriately in a given context? Can the employee describe the characteristics of the situation and how competing values were balanced? What was the outcome? Though such an approach may not be new, through the lens of leadership it becomes possible to see and evaluate the exercise of discretion and judge its appropriateness.

Such approaches, at least in part, are also more consistent with recent political and other pressures on public organizations to develop measures of program outcomes in addition to the more traditional procedural measures of performance. In the street-level leadership model, both are important. In the context of evaluating individual workers, however, the notion of "outcome" must be considered to include such factors as the outcomes for the participants and the ability of workers to handle situations without making problems worse. For example, a positive outcome may be that the participants in a potential street fight were not arrested because the officer defused the situation and had a constructive interaction with the participants. Evaluations must acknowledge this, not simply count the number of arrests an officer makes and note the speed with which the relevant paperwork is filed.

In changing how street-level public servants are evaluated, it is also necessary to acknowledge and reinforce the increasing leadership responsibilities that are being given to workers. Most current evaluation systems implicitly communicate to workers that their most important responsibility is to adhere to procedures and complete paperwork on time. This creates a significant disjunction between the realities of street-level public service and the organization's official charge to workers. The reality is that worker discretion is substantial and inevitable. Accounting for paperwork and checking to see if procedures were followed are important and necessary. But if that is all that is done, important parts of these workers' jobs are being ignored. Expanding the evaluation process to include assessment of workers' discretionary decisions is crucial if agencies are to encourage workers to implement programs in ways that manifest the department's values along with those of the broader community. Systems of evaluation need to be revamped, then, both to encourage the use of legitimate discretion and to check abuses of discretion and channel it into more acceptable paths.

Changing how these workers are supervised goes hand-in-hand with changing and broadening how they are evaluated. At the most basic level, supervisors need to think of and treat workers as street-level leaders. Supervisors should expect workers to understand and advance programmatic and community goals, to sensitively and appropriately assess and respond to situations, and to take responsibility for their choices. Conversely, then, workers can reasonably expect their supervisors to treat them in a manner that recognizes their more immediate and direct vantage point for evaluating and responding to situations and problems on the street. Workers should also be able to expect supervisors to talk through cases with them, to listen to how they assessed the situation, and to support them if they can legitimate their choices. When possible and appropriate, they should be consulted about procedural and other changes in their departments. Street-level leaders should be managed and treated, then, as important resources and responsible decision makers who will be held accountable for their choices.

These types of supervisory approaches are certainly nothing revolutionary. In fact, they probably represent what most would consider to be conventional standards for good management in contemporary organizational settings. It is important to emphasize, however, that they are not discussed here as management tools per se. Rather, they are highlighted as natural consequences of changing how supervisors and organizational managers *think* about these workers. It is that shift in thinking that is more important than the use of any particular supervisory technique.

Along these lines, another change that is likely to be necessary if departments are to foster street-level leadership is a reconsideration of the nature and types of rewards given to workers. Recognition of their public-service contribution, for example, appears to be critical. Many workers voiced a desire for management to be more involved and to appreciate how they were helping people.

One worker put it simply: "I want credit for what I do. I want recognition." While workload pressure may require workers to deal with issues and problems as quickly as practicable, recognition for helping people can still be provided. These workers believe strongly that the work they do is important, and they want their agencies to acknowledge that it is so. Further, well-meaning supervisors who insist on conformity to narrowly defined, inflexible roles may create frustration and the perception that management does not understand or appreciate what they do. Leaders find satisfaction in ways different from those typically associated with bureaucrats, and agencies need to acknowledge this as they work to develop street-level leaders.

Cumulatively, similar changes at the departmental level can be expected to help develop workers who are creative, flexible, and aware of both the department's mission and the goals of the community the agency serves. Such workers, then, can help the department to fulfill its mission and provide public services more effectively. Recruitment, training, supervision, and evaluation all need to reflect a recognition of the complex and important work street-level leaders do. To the degree that this consistency in orientation is achieved, street-level leadership can be more effectively realized.

Changing Governance

It will be difficult to develop street-level leadership unless the idea of workers as leaders gains currency within the broader governance system. As suggested in Chapter One, society holds contradictory expectations about worker discretion. While there are many forces which encourage the expansion of worker discretion, many argue that discretion ought to be constrained. Some resurrect the politics/administration dichotomy, arguing that bureaucratic discretion is inconsistent with democratic ideals. Others argue against discretion because they disagree with a particular discretionary choice or set of choices. Indeed, given the potential for the abuse of discretion, it is probably easier to argue in favor of limiting discretion than it is to support the notion that workers ought to actively use it, but use it appropriately and legitimately. Within the governance system, then, there are strong pressures that discourage the creation of street-level leadership.

As a consequence, changing basic assumptions about what street-level workers do and how what they do fits within the governance process will be challenging. One of the primary barriers to doing so is the assumption, well-established in the popular culture, that all bureaucrats are incompetent and that government itself is synonymous with waste and abuse. It is important to note, however, that this has not always been the case. Even as recently as the early 1960s, popular depictions of public servants were generally quite positive. In the last twenty-five years, however, we have gone from Miss Brooks and Joe Friday to a much darker picture of renegade cops, uncaring social-service workers, and bungling bureaucrats. But beyond these media images, at least part of the negative shift in public perception can be attributed to political leaders who have demonized bureaucracies in the name of ideology and political gain. Twenty-five years of emphasis on the negative dimensions of bureaucracy, in combination with actual errors made by agencies and workers themselves, have tended to encourage citizens to be skeptical of bureaucracies and their employees.

But the image of public employees as lazy, incompetent, and uncaring is not necessarily a "given." Rather, it is a barrier which can and must be overcome if sound, effective governance is to be realized. Moreover, it is not a hopeless proposition. As Hart (1987), Kernell (1986), and Tulis (1987), among others, have noted, it is possible for political leaders to use their powers of public persuasion to support new ideas, attitudes, and expectations. If political leaders promote the idea of street-level leadership as a means to achieve a government that works better, it can be expected that public attitudes will change over time. Additionally, to the extent that negative public images of public employees are related to the actual mistakes and errors made by agencies and their workers, helping workers to behave as street-level leaders can be expected to result in more favorable public attitudes over time. In this way, the development of more positive public attitudes and the work of street-level leaders become mutually reinforcing. In the simplest sense, leaders need followers and followers need leaders. In the same way, street-level public servants need citizens to do their jobs, and citizens need street-level public servants to accomplish community objectives.

There are a number of other changes at the governance level that can support workers in striving toward this ideal. Again, while these ideas are nothing new, they are important in supporting and enhancing the practice of street-level leadership. For example, to the extent that lawmakers can clarify the intent and objectives of legislation, it enhances the understanding of those objectives by the street-level leaders who must make frontline decisions to achieve them. Further, in some cases, the law may need to be changed to grant *additional* discretion to agencies and workers. Some legislation, by detailing the ways in which programs are to be implemented, has the effect of constraining worker and agency discretion to the detriment of the goals being sought.

Resource considerations will also, in some cases, be important. Legislative support for training and the redesign of worker-evaluation systems, for example, may be necessary. Additional resources may also be needed in recruiting and retaining the types of people who are likely to be effective street-level leaders. Greater emphasis on establishing linkages among agencies treating similar cases may also be useful since, as a practical matter, cases of child abuse can include other issues like drug dependency, family violence, or more "hard" crimes. In some instances, at least in the short term, leadership training and development may be a resource-intensive process. However, such investments can reasonably be expected to produce and support street-level leaders who can more effectively meet public objectives.

Thus, it is important to think about changing the ways in which the governance system authorizes, supports, evaluates, and engages street-level leaders as they do their jobs. If citizens, communities, and workers join together in pursuit of common goals, in combination with the changes in individual workers and agencies discussed above, the full potential of street-level leaders can realized.

THE LIMITATIONS OF STREET-LEVEL LEADERSHIP

Having just argued that there are substantial advantages to viewing workers as leaders, and having outlined a number of changes that could be made to support the development of street-level leaders, it must be admitted that there are limitations inherent in the model. Some of these limitations are innate to this study's methodology; others lie in the nature of social/political life in the United States; and yet others lie in the types of problems that street-level public servants deal with. Street-level leadership is a tool, not a panacea, in the struggle to solve public problems.

At a somewhat technical level, the model of street-level leadership was based on observations from a particular set of workers who may not be, and probably are not, representative of the public service in its entirety. These workers were on the front line, and their work was qualitatively different than that which a clerk or an analyst might do. Accordingly, the model of street-level leadership may not be applicable to all public servants.

Moreover, as was indicated in Table 1 in Chapter Three, not all work performed by frontline public servants can be understood as leadership. There are many circumstances, like murder-scene investigations and the carrying out of court orders, in which discretion can and ought to be constrained. While much of the work observed for this project was leadership, much was not. It is important to attend to this difference if street-level leadership is implemented in relevant social-service agencies.

More broadly, street-level public servants work in a complex system of checks and balances, of which they are only one part. Workers may desire to achieve certain goals and may do a great deal of creative "leg work" to support their plans, but if prosecutors, courts, legislators, agencies, or citizens at large do not support these workers, they cannot succeed. Indeed, since supervisors, agencies, prosecutors, courts, and legislators have significantly more power to influence events than do individual workers, such opposition is virtually guaranteed to lead to failure on workers' parts. Street-level leadership thus requires the interactive support of diverse parts of the governance system and, in its absence, is unlikely to work.

Maybe most importantly, for all the potential power of the street-level leadership model, it is not a complete answer to all the problems in public service. As we frequently tell our students, if the problems of government were easy to fix, they would have been fixed by now. Intractable and "wicked" social problems are not going to be eliminated simply because workers respond to them as leaders. It is unrealistic to believe that street-level leaders, as one component in a complex system of program definition, delivery, and assessment, can resolve problems that have remained with us for decades. Instead, what will change is the way workers, agencies, clients, and communities think about roles and responsibilities in responding to these problems. Further, ways of accounting for success and failure will also change to reflect the motives, goals, and values that are manifested in workers' actions.

Street-level leadership, then, is not "the" answer to resolving the complex problems that exist in contemporary society. Street-level leaders can no more definitively solve them than stop the tides. Instead, what can be anticipated is a new way of working on such problems that is grounded in core values and ideals. Working from this foundation can encourage decisions that are responsive to both the needs of the clients being served and the broader community's need to retain accountability over worker exercise of discretion.

CONCLUSION

Though there will always be tension between the concepts of bureaucracy and democracy, the notion of leadership provides a means by which the values of the two can be reconciled in a model of public service. Encouraging public servants to embrace and address the values that underlie public programs is consistent with the realities of contemporary practice and the principles of democratic governance. As street-level leaders, public servants are part of a system of laws, values, moral standards, and interests that influence their actions. Discretion is not merely an autonomous act taken by an individual bureaucrat; rather, it is an act of organizational, political, and social leadership, and ought to be accounted for as such.

E. E. Schattschneider is credited with saying that theory is "the shortest way of saying something important" (1968, 128). It is our hope that in developing a new model of public service, we have said something important. Viewing public servants as street-level leaders will require a profound change in the public's understanding of what public employees do, why what they do matters, and what the meaning of bureaucratic discretion is in the broader political system. Words are extremely powerful, however. By changing the vocabulary we use, the role of public servants can be understood and communicated differently, the framework for training public servants to meet new challenges and standards can be strengthened, and the exercise of discretion can be judged in the context of democratic governance. Then, potentially, the individuals who do these important and difficult jobs will be able to meet their, and our, goals more effectively.

In the end, it is street-level public servants who make politics real for ordinary citizens. Whatever debates occur in legislatures, courts, agencies, or the media about the purposes of different pro-grams, eventually such conversations are reduced to the relation-ship between police officers, social-service workers, or other public servants and their clients. It is the decisions those workers make in the specific circumstances they face that will ultimately define how ordinary citizens experience public policies.

The power to make politics meaningful for citizens puts street-level public servants in a central position in the governance sys-tem. Their decisions and actions can work to either augment or undermine citizens' trust and support of the political system. It is for this reason that this book has focused on these workers so extensively. As so many workers explained, always using different words but meaning the same thing, theirs is a difficult job. Sup-porting these workers, and finding ways to help them do their jobs better, is vital to our future.

Appendix

For the most part, the workers observed for this book worked in one of four agencies: 1) Huntsville, AL, Police Department; 2) Spokane County, WA, Sheriff's Department; 3) Illinois Department of Children and Family Services, Bloomington, IL; and 4) Arizona Department of Economic Security, Phoenix, AZ. This appendix provides more detailed information with regard to these organizations and the areas they serve.

The Huntsville, AL, Police Department serves a midsized, geographically spread out, economically and racially diverse city in northern Alabama. Huntsville, according to 1990 U.S. Census data, has approximately 160,000 residents. Its median household income in 1989 was $32,300. Huntsville's 1989 per capita income was high compared to the other communities under study, at $16,200 (U.S. Census 1990). Its population is 72 percent white and 25 percent African-American; 3 percent of its citizens define themselves as members of other races.

This brief demographic sketch only partially captures Huntsville's diversity, however. It is, in many ways, a government town—over 19,000 of its citizens work directly for various federal, state, and local government entities (U.S. Census 1990). Additionally, many of the companies that form Huntsville's economic base are associated with the National Aeronautic and Space Administration's (NASA) Marshall Space Flight Center and the U.S. Army's Redstone Arsenal. In many ways, in fact, Huntsville is a model "new South" city built on information and high-technology industries.

Side by side with sophisticated technology and other industries, however, stand pockets of striking poverty and economic decay. Like many other Southern cities, Huntsville is significantly segregated by both race and class—there are clearly definable poor, middle-class, and wealthy areas that are generally racially homogeneous. The wealth that Huntsville produces, then, is not evenly distributed throughout the city.

The Huntsville Police Department's Patrol Division serves this diverse city in three shifts averaging approximately sixty officers each. Officers generally patrol relatively small zones in which they are expected to provide primary police services such as answering calls, checking buildings for burglaries, and other functions. As a rule, officer response times within their patrol zones are intended to be quick, and officers are generally able to expect backup support to arrive soon after they request it. While patrol zones are smaller in areas where calls for service are more frequent, thereby facilitating more patrols and faster response times, every part of the city is covered on a regular basis by patrol officers.

The Spokane County, WA, Sheriff's Department, in contrast, serves a very different constituency in a very different environment. Spokane County is over 1,700 square miles in area, making it larger than the state of Rhode Island. It has two major population centers: 1) the city of Spokane, which is served by its own police force; and 2) the Spokane Valley, an unincorporated concentration of over 140,000 people just east of the city of Spokane. The county, minus the city, has a total population of approximately 184,000 (U.S. Census 1990). About 96 percent of its residents are white; African-Americans make up barely 1 percent of the county's population, and members of other groups, primarily Native Americans, make up the remainder (U.S. Census 1990). In 1989, its median household income was $25,800—almost $7,000 less than Huntsville's. Per capita income in Spokane County in 1989 was $12,800 (U.S. Census 1990).

Whereas Huntsville can be characterized by its high-tech economic base, as well as by its striking contrasts of poverty and wealth, Spokane County is a much more homogeneous area. Its economic base is light industrial—there are major aluminum and aircraft parts manufacturing operations there, and Fairchild Air Force Base is a major employer. To the extent that there is diversity, it is more geographic than economic or ethnic. Eastern Spokane County is comparatively green and mountainous, while the western part of the county is a high desert with gently rolling hills covered, for the most part, by wheat fields.

The Spokane County Sheriff's Department provides primary police protection to the parts of Spokane County not incorporated into the city of Spokane. It concentrates its resources in the population center of the Spokane Valley, but with between eight and fourteen deputies on a given shift, even in the valley it may take deputies ten to fifteen minutes to respond to a service call. Other patrol areas may encompass literally hundreds of square miles. Response times to calls for service in such zones may exceed an hour, and it is possible for backup to be an additional hour away. It is in fact common for some areas of the county to be essentially unpatrolled for days and weeks at a time. Unlike officers in the heavily supported Huntsville Police Department, then, Spokane County deputies often work isolated from both their supervisors and their fellow officers.

Taken together, the Huntsville Police Department and the Spokane County Sheriff's Department serve as a useful sample of a wide range of environments of police activity. Huntsville is a comparatively wealthy, racially diverse urban area in which police response times are relatively quick. Spokane County is a less wealthy, less diverse, more rural community in which police response to calls for service is generally much longer. To the degree that such variables can be seen to shape what police officers do, the contrasts between these departments yield useful insights into how officers make the decisions they do. In addition, to the degree that Huntsville and Spokane County are representative of a range of communities around the United States, any insights derived from this research ought to be generalizable.

The observations conducted with social-service workers provided a distribution of geographic, economic, and racial diversity similar to that which was generated during the research with police agencies. The Bloomington field office of the Illinois Department of Children and Family Services, for example, covers a three-county area that includes substantial urban and rural populations. Combined, the three counties total 184,900 residents with a 1989 median household income of $29,600 and an average per capita income of $13,100 (U.S. Census 1990).

This demographic depiction of the three counties served by the Bloomington field office misses much of the diversity in the area, however. McLean County, where Bloomington is located, is a large, wealthy urban center that holds the world headquarters of State Farm Insurance Companies; Illinois State and Illinois Wesleyan

Universities; and major manufacturing operations for Mitsubishi, Eureka, and Beer Nuts. Its population is 129,200, almost 70 percent of the tricounty area's total (U.S. Census 1990). Additionally, its 1989 median household and per capita incomes of $31,400 and $14,100, respectively, were significantly higher than those in the other two counties (U.S. Census 1990).

By contrast, DeWitt County has a total population of 16,500; only 60 of its residents were African-American (U.S. Census 1990). Whereas only 25 percent of McLean County's residents lived in a rural environment, 55 percent of DeWitt County's citizens did (U.S. Census 1990). DeWitt County also lacks any major industrial or technological economic base; its 1989 median household and per capita incomes were accordingly much lower than McLean County's at $27,200 and $12,900 each (U.S. Census 1990).

Livingston County, the third county covered by the Bloomington field office, stands numerically in between McLean and DeWitt County numbers: fully 7 percent of its 39,300 residents were either African-American or of other races; its median household income was $29,800; its per capita income was $12,120; and its population splits almost exactly 50–50 urban/rural (U.S. Census 1990). It lacks a substantial industrial or technological economic base; however, a major state prison is located there, guaranteeing a substantial infusion of state money.

In striking contrast with Bloomington, IL, and its three-county scope, Phoenix, AZ, and its surrounding communities constitute one of the major metropolitan areas in the United States. Almost two million people live there, and, with the exception of Huntsville, AL, it is the most ethnically and racially diverse of any community examined in this research: 85 percent of its residents are white and 4 percent are African-American; 16 percent are of Hispanic origin (U.S. Census 1990). Its 1989 median household and per capita incomes were $30,500 and $15,000, respectively, making it among the wealthier areas studied (U.S. Census 1990).

Along with being the state capital, Phoenix has a diverse economic base dominated by service industries, retail stores, manufacturing, and financial/insurance/banking institutions. Because the Phoenix area, at the time of the study, was one of the most rapidly growing areas of the United States, the construction business was also a major part of the local economy. Like many other urban areas, it has residential areas that can be characterized as wealthy and exclusive, middle-class, and quite poor. Also, one of the distinct features of Phoenix is its climate. While the temperatures are usually moderate from midfall through the early spring, the summers are long and very hot. This creates problems for clients who may lack housing or the financial resources for air conditioning. It also is a negative environmental element for workers who must spend many hours conducting investigations and dealing with sometimes emotionally charged situations while driving cars that must be left out in the sun and then going into homes and buildings that lack cooling systems.

In the state of Arizona, Child Protective Services, Adult Protective Services, and Developmental Disabilities (along with several other organizational units) are housed within an umbrella state social-service agency—the Arizona Department of Economic Security. While these units serve the entire state, the observations for this study were all conducted within the Phoenix metropolitan area. In addition to the City of Phoenix, this included Tempe, Chandler, Mesa, Scottsdale, Glendale, and Paradise Valley.

Cumulatively, the diversity of the agencies studied, the communities they served, and the environments in which they operated provides a useful database on which to build and test the model of street-level leadership presented in this book. To the degree that such diversity shapes what workers do and the demands they face, the model's ability to account for this diversity speaks to its applicability across a wide range of agencies, communities, and environments.

References

Alexander, R., and C. Alexander. 1995. Criminal prosecution of child welfare workers. *Social Work* 40: 809–814.

Argyris, C. 1955. Some characteristics of successful executives. *Personnel Journal* (June): 50–63.

———. 1964. *Integrating the individual and the organization.* New York: John Wiley.

Atwater, L. 1988. The relative importance of situational and individual variables in predicting leader behavior: The surprising impact of subordinate trust. *Group and Organization Studies* 13 (3): 290–310.

Austin, D. 1992. Community policing: The critical partnership. *Public Management* 74: 3–9.

Ayman, R., M. Chemers, and F. Fiedler. 1995. The contingency model of leadership effectiveness: Its levels of analysis. *Leadership Quarterly* 6 (2): 147–167.

Barth, T. 1992. The public interest and administrative discretion. *American Review of Public Administration* 22 (4): 289–300.

Bass, B. 1960. *Leadership, psychology, and organizational behavior.* New York: Harper and Brothers.

———. 1990. *Handbook of leadership: A survey of theory and research.* New York: Free Press.

Bellavita, C. 1991. The public administrator as hero. *Administration & Society* 23 (2): 155–185.

Bennis, W. 1984. The four competencies of leadership. *Training and Development Journal* (August): 14–90.

Bernstein, B., and B. McCutchan. 1983. The grand jury v. the social workers: Friends or enemies? *Social Work* 28: 224–227.

Bierstedt, R. 1950. An analysis of social power. *American Sociological Review* 15: 730–736.

Blake, R., and J. Mouton. 1964. *The managerial grid.* Houston: Gulf Publishing.

Brashears, F. 1995. Supervision as social work practice. *Social Work* 40: 692–699.

Brieland, D. 1995. Social work practice: History and evolution. In *Encyclopedia of Social Work*, edited by R. Edwards and J. Hopps, 19 (3): 2247–2257. Washington, DC: National Association of Social Workers Press.

Brown, L. 1989. Community policing: A practical guide for police officials. *Perspectives on Policing* 12: 1–11.

Burns, J. M. 1978. *Leadership*. New York: Harper and Row.

Carlyle, T. 1840. *On heroes and hero worship and the heroic in society*. London: Chapman and Hall.

Carroll, J. 1995. The rhetoric of reform and political reality in the national performance review. *Public Administration Review* 55 (3): 302–312.

Cooper, T. 1991. *An ethic of citizenship for public administration*. Englewood Cliffs, NJ: Prentice-Hall.

Crothers, L., and J. Vinzant. 1994. Discretion and street-level leadership in law enforcement. Paper presented at the annual meeting of the Western Political Science Association, Albuquerque, NM.

Crouch, A., and P. Yetton. 1987. Manager behavior, leadership style, and subordinate performance: An empirical extension of Vroom-Yetton conflict rule. *Organizational Behavior and Human Decision Processes* 39: 384–396.

Dahl, R. 1957. The concept of power. *Behavioral Science* 2: 201–215.

Delattre, E. 1989. *Character and cops*. Washington, DC: American Enterprise Institute for Public Policy Research.

Denhardt, R. 1984. *Theories of public organization*. Belmont, CA: Brooks/Cole.

DeSantis, V., and S. Durst. 1996. Comparing job satisfaction among public- and private-sector employees. *American Review of Public Administration* 26 (3): 327–343.

Douglas, M. 1970. *Natural symbols: Explorations in cosmology*. London: Barrie and Rockliff.

———. 1982. Cultural bias. In *In the Active Voice*, edited by M. Douglas, 183–254. London: Routledge and Kegan Paul.

Downs, A. 1967. *Inside bureaucracy*. Boston: Little, Brown.

Edley, C. 1990. *Administrative law: Rethinking judicial control of bureaucracy*. New Haven: Yale University Press.

Fenno, R. 1978. *Home style: House members in their districts*. Glenview, IL: Scott, Foresman and Company.

Fiedler, F. 1970. The contingency model: A theory of leadership effectiveness. In *Classic readings in organizational behavior*, 2nd. ed., edited by J. S. Ott (1996): 198–209. Belmont, CA: Wadsworth.

Fiedler, F., and M. Chemers. 1982. *Improving leadership effectiveness: The leader match concept*, 2nd ed. New York: John Wiley.

Fox, C. 1996. Reinventing government as postmodern symbolic politics. *Public Administration Review* 56 (3): 256–262.

Franklin, D. 1985. Differential clinical assessments: The influence of class and race. *Social Service Review* 59: 44–61.

Franz, V., and D. Jones. 1987. Perceptions of organizational performance in suburban police departments: A critique of the military model. *Journal of Police Science and Administration* 5: 153–161.

Frederickson, H. G. 1971. Toward a new public administration. In *Classics of public administration*, 2nd ed., edited by J. Shafritz and A. Hyde (1987): 424–439. Chicago, IL: The Dorsey Press.

———. 1996. Comparing the reinventing government movement with new public administration. *Public Administration Review* 56 (3): 263–270.

Friedmann, R. 1992. *Community policing: Comparative perspectives and prospects*. New York: St. Martin's Press.

Friedrich, C. 1963. *The philosophy of law in historical perspective*, 2nd ed. Chicago: University of Chicago Press.

Galton, F. 1869. *Hereditary genius*. London: Macmillan.

Gardner, J. 1990. *On leadership*. New York: The Free Press.

Geertz, C. 1977. The judging of nations: Some comments on the assessment of regimes in the new states. *European Journal of Sociology* 18 (2): 245–261.

Geier, J. 1967. A trait approach to the study of leadership. *Journal of Communication* 17: 316–323.

Giddens, A. 1976. *New rules of sociological method*. New York: Basic Books.

Glaser, B., and A. Strauss. 1967. *The discovery of grounded theory: Strategies for qualitative research*. London: Wiedenfeld and Nicholson.

Goldstein, H. 1990. *Problem-oriented policing*. New York: McGraw-Hill.

Golembiewski, R. 1989. Toward a positive and practical public management: Organizational research supporting a fourth critical citizenship. *Administration and Society* 21 (2): 200–227.

Goodnow, F. 1900. Politics and administration. In *Classics of public administration*, 2nd ed., edited by J. Shafritz & A. Hyde (1987): 26–29. Chicago: The Dorsey Press.

Goodsell, C. 1980. Client evaluation of three welfare programs. *Administration and Society* 12: 123–136.

———. 1990. Emerging issues in public administration. In *Public administration: The state of the discipline*, edited by N. Lynn and A. Wildavsky: 495–507. Chatham, NJ: Chatham House Publishers.

Gore, A. 1994. *Creating a government that works better & costs less: Status report, September 1994*. Washington, DC: U.S. Government Printing Office.

Green, C., and C. Schriesheim. 1980. Leader-group interactions: A longitudinal field investigation. *Journal of Applied Psychology* 65 (1): 50–59.

Green, R., L. Keller, and G. Wamsley. 1993. Reconstituting a profession for American public administration. *Public Administration Review* 53 (6): 516–524.

Greller, M. 1980. Evaluation of feedback sources as a function of role and organizational level. *Journal of Applied Psychology* 65 (1): 24–27.

Guyot, D. 1991. Problem-oriented policing shines in the stats. *Public Management* 73: 12–16.

Hargrove, E., and J. Glidewell, eds. 1990. *Impossible jobs in public management*. Lawrence, KS: University Press of Kansas.

Harmon, M. 1990. The responsible actor as "tortured soul": The case of Horatio Hornblower. In *Images and identities in public administration*, edited by H. Kass and B. Catron: 113–130. Newbury Park, CA: Sage Publications.

Harmon, M., and R. Mayer. 1986. *Organization theory for public administration*. Boston: Little, Brown and Company.

Harrison, E., and M. Pelletier. 1987. Perceptions of bureaucratization, role performance, and organizational effectiveness in a metropolitan police department. *Journal of Police Science and Administration* 15: 262–270.

Hart, R. 1987. *The sound of leadership: Presidential communication in the modern age.* Chicago: University of Chicago Press.

Hegar, R. 1988. Legal and social work approaches to sibling separation in foster care. *Child Welfare* 67: 113–121.

Hersey, P., and K. Blanchard. 1988. *Management of organizational behavior,* 5th ed. Englewood Cliffs, NJ: Prentice Hall.

Hersey, P., K. Blanchard, and D. Johnson. 1996. *Management of organizational behavior,* 7th ed. Upper Saddle River, NJ: Prentice Hall.

Hodges, D., and R. Durant. 1989. The professional state revisited: Twixt Scylla and Charybdis? *Public Administration Review* 48 (5): 474–484.

Hoffmann, J. 1980. Problems of access in the study of social elites and boards of directors. In *Fieldwork experience: Qualitative approaches to social research,* edited by W. Shaffir, R. Stebbins, and A. Turowetz, 45–56. New York: St. Martin's Press.

Hopps, J., and P. Collins. 1995. Social work profession overview. In *Encyclopedia of Social Work,* edited by R. Edwards and J. Hopps, 19 (3): 2267–2282. Washington, DC: National Association of Social Workers Press.

House, R. 1971. A path-goal theory of leader effectiveness. *Administrative Sciences Quarterly* 16: 321–339.

House, R., A. Filley, and D. Gujarati. 1971. Leadership style, hierarchical influence, and the satisfaction of subordinate role expectations: A test of Likert's influence proposition. *Journal of Applied Psychology* 55: 422–432.

House, R., and T. Mitchell. 1974. Path–goal theory of leadership. *Contemporary Business* 3 (Fall): 81–98.

Howing, P., and J. Wodarski. 1992. Legal requisites for social workers in child abuse and neglect situations. *Social Work* 37: 330–336.

Jackman, R. 1993. *Power without force: The political capacity of nation-states.* Ann Arbor, MI: University of Michigan Press.

Jago, A., and V. Vroom. 1980. An evaluation of two alternatives to the Vroom/Yetton normative model. *Academy of Management Journal* 23: 347–355.

Johnson, J. 1975. *Doing field research.* New York: The Free Press.

Johnson, J., and R. Joslyn. 1986. *Political science research methods.* Washington, DC: CQ Press.

Jorgensen, D. 1989. *Participant observation: A methodology for human studies.* Newbury Park, CA: Sage.

Jos, P. 1990. Administrative responsibility revisited: Moral consensus and moral autonomy. *Administration & Society* 22 (2): 228–248.

Kadushin, A. 1985. *Supervision in social work*. 2nd ed. New York: Columbia University Press.

Kaplan, A. n.d. *The conduct of inquiry: Methodology for behavioral science*. New York: Harper and Row.

Kass, H. 1990. Stewardship as fundamental element in images of public administration. In *Images and identities in public administration*, edited by H. Kass and B. Catron: 113–130. Newbury Park, CA: Sage Publications.

Kaufman, H. 1960. *The forest ranger: A study in administrative behavior*. Baltimore: Johns Hopkins Press.

Kearney, R., and C. Sinha. 1988. Professionalism and bureaucratic responsiveness: Conflict or compatibility. *Public Administration Review* 47 (1): 571–579.

Kelly, M. 1994. Theories of justice and street-level discretion. *Journal of Public Administration Research and Theory* 4: 119–140.

Kernell, S. 1986. *Going public: New strategies of presidential leadership*. Washington, DC: CQ Press.

Kirkpatrick, S.A., and E.A. Locke. 1991. Leadership: Do traits matter? *Executive* 5 (2): 48–60.

Kirlin, J., and R. Thompson. 1987. Political institutions: Adaptability and paralysis. In *The capacity to respond*, edited by T. Bradshaw and C. Bell: 73–93. Berkeley, California: Institute of Governmental Studies.

Kroeger, N. 1975. Bureaucracy, social exchange, and benefits received in a public assistance agency. *Social Problems* 23: 182–196.

Kutchens, H. 1991. The fiduciary relationship: The legal basis for social workers' responsibilities to clients. *Social Work* 36: 106–113.

Lee, R., and R. Hull. 1983. Legal, casework, and ethical obligations in "risk adoption." *Child Welfare* 62: 150–454.

Lewin, K., R. Lippitt, and R. White. 1939. Patterns of aggressive behavior in experimentally created social climates. *Journal of Social Psychology* 10: 271–301.

Likert, R. 1961. *New patterns of management*. New York: McGraw-Hill.

———. 1967. *The human organization: Its management and value*. New York: McGraw-Hill.

Linders, S., and B. Peters. 1987. A design perspective on policy implementation: The fallacies of misplaced prescriptions. *Policy Studies Review* 6 (3): 459–475.

Lipsky, M. 1980. *Street-level bureaucracy: Dilemmas of the individual in public services*. New York, NY: Russell Sage.

Lopata, H. 1980. Interviewing American widows. In *Fieldwork experience: Qualitative approaches to social research*, edited by W. Shaffir, R. Stebbins, and A. Turowetz: 68–81. New York: St. Martin's Press.

Lovrich, N. 1981. Professional ethics and the public interest: Sources of judgment. *Public Personnel Management Journal* 10 (January): 87–92.

Lukes, Steven. 1974. *Power: A radical view*. London: Macmillan.

Lutrin, C., and A. Settle. 1992. *American public administration: Concepts and cases*, 4th ed. St. Paul, MN: West Publishing.

Magill, R. 1979. *Community decision making for social welfare*. New York: Human Sciences Press.

McCurdy, H. 1986. *Public administration: A bibliographic guide to the literature*. New York, NY: Marcel Dekker.

Merriam-Webster, Incorporated. 1996. *Merriam-Webster's Collegiate Dictionary*, 10th ed. Springfield, MA: Merriam-Webster.

Mills, C., and W. Bohannon. 1980. Personality characteristics of effective state police officers. *Journal of Applied Psychology* 65 (6): 680–684.

Morgan, D. 1990. Administrative phronesis: Discretion and the problem of administrative legitimacy in our constitutional system. In *Images and identities in public administration*, edited by H. Kass and B. Catron: 67–86. Newbury Park, CA: Sage Publications.

Morrow, W. 1980. *Public administration: Politics, policy, and the political system*, 2nd ed. New York: Random House.

Mosher, F. 1968. *Democracy and the public service*. New York: Oxford University Press.

Muir, W. 1977. *Police: Street corner politicians*. Chicago: University of Chicago Press.

Nahavandi, A. 1997. *The art and science of leadership*. Upper Saddle River, NJ: Prentice Hall.

Nakamura, R. 1988. The textbook policy process and implementation research. *Policy Studies Review* 7 (1): 142–154.

Neugeboren, B. 1996. *Environmental practice in the human services: Integration of micro and macro roles, skills, and contexts*. New York: Haworth Press.

Neustadt, R. 1986. *Presidential power: The politics of leadership from FDR to Carter*. New York: Macmillan Publishing Company.

Newland, C., ed. 1980. *Professional public executives*. Washington, DC: American Society of Public Administration.

O'Looney, J. 1996. *Redesigning the work of human services*. Westport, CT: Quorum Books.

Ott, J. S., ed. 1989. *Classic readings in organizational behavior*. Belmont, California: Brooks/Cole.

Peters, L., D. Hartke, and J. Pohlmann. 1985. Fiedler's contingency theory of leadership: An application of the meta-analysis procedure of Schmitt and Hunter. *Psychological Bulletin* 97: 274–285.

Peyrot, M. 1982. Caseload management: Choosing suitable clients in a community health clinic agency. *Social Problems* 30: 157–167.

Popple, P. 1995. Social work profession: History. In *Encyclopedia of Social Work*, edited by R. Edwards and J. Hopps 19 (3): 2282–2292. Washington, DC: National Association of Social Workers Press.

Pressman, J., and A. Wildavsky. 1973. *Implementation: How great expectations in Washington are dashed in Oakland*. Berkeley: University of California Press.

Pugh, G. 1986. The good police officer: Qualities, roles and concepts. *Journal of Police Science and Administration* 14: 1–5.

Rashomon. 1951. Japan. Daie Motion Picture Company.

Reamer, F. 1994. *Social work malpractice and liability: Strategies for prevention.* New York: Columbia University Press.

Reuss-Ianni, E., and F. A. Ianni. 1983. Street cops and management cops: The two cultures of policing. In *Control in the Police Organization,* edited by M. Punch: 251–274. Cambridge, MA: MIT Press.

Rohr, J. 1986. *To run a Constitution: The legitimacy of the administrative state.* Lawrence, KS: University Press of Kansas.

Rosenbloom, D., and J. Carroll. 1990. *Toward constitutional competence: A casebook for public administrators.* Englewood Cliffs, NJ: Prentice Hall.

Ross, J., and M. Ross. 1974. Participant observation in political research. *Political Methodology* 1: 65–66.

Russell, B. 1938. *Power: A new social analysis.* New York: W. W. Norton and Company.

Sank, L. 1974. Effective and ineffective managerial traits obtained in naturalistic descriptions from executive members from a super-corporation. *Personnel Psychology* 19: 275–286.

Sayre, W. 1958. Premises of public administration: Past and emerging. *Public Administration Review* 18 (2): 102–105.

Schattschneider, E. E. 1968. Quoted in S. Bailey, Objectives of the theory of public administration. In *Theory and practice of public administration: Scope, objectives, and methods,* edited by J. Charlesworth. Philadelphia: The American Academy of Political and Social Science.

Schein, E. 1992. *Organizational culture and leadership.* San Francisco: Jossey-Bass.

Schroeder, L. 1995. *The legal environment of social work.* Washington, DC: NASW Press.

Scott, P. 1997. Assessing determinants of bureaucratic discretion: An experiment in street-level decision making. *Journal of Public Administration Research and Theory* 7 (1): 35–37.

Seltzer, J., and R. Numerof. 1988. Supervisory leadership and subordinate burnout. *Academy of Management Journal* 31: 439–446.

Shafritz, J. 1988. *The Dorsey dictionary of politics and government.* Chicago: The Dorsey Press.

Sieber, J., ed. 1982. *The ethics of social research.* New York: Springer-Verlag.

Skolnick, J., and J. Fyfe. 1993. *Above the law: Police and the excessive use of force.* New York: Free Press.

Sparrow, M. 1988. Implementing community policing. *Perspectives on Policing* 9. Washington, DC: National Institute of Justice.

Spicer, M. 1990. A contractarian approach to public administration. *Administration & Society* 22 (3): 303–316.

Spicer, M., and L. Terry. 1993. Legitimacy, history, and logic: Public administration and the Constitution. *Public Administration Review* 53 (3): 239–246.

Stinson, J., and R. Johnson. 1975. The path goal theory of leadership: A partial test and suggested refinement. *Academy of Management Journal* 18: 242–252.

Stogdill, R. 1974. *Handbook of leadership: A survey of the literature.* New York: Free Press.

Stone, C. 1981. Attitudinal tendencies among officials. In *The public encounter: Where state and citizen meet,* edited by C. Goodsell. Bloomington: Indiana University Press.

Terry, L. 1990. Leadership in the administrative state: The concept of administrative conservatorship. *Administration & Society* 21 (4): 395–412.

Thibault, E., L. Lynch, and R. McBride. 1990. *Proactive police management,* 2nd ed. Englewood Cliffs, NJ: Prentice Hall.

Thompson, M., R. Ellis, and A. Wildavsky. 1990. *Cultural theory.* Boulder, CO: Westview Press.

Ting, Y. 1996. Analysis of job satisfaction of the federal white-collar work force: Findings from the survey of federal employees. *American Review of Public Administration* (26) 4: 440–456.

Toren, N. 1975. *Social work: The case of a semi-profession.* Beverly Hills: Sage Publications.

Trojanowicz, R., and M. Moore. 1988. The meaning of community in community policing. *Community Policing Series* 15. East Lansing, MI: Michigan State University Press.

Tulis, J. 1987. *The rhetorical presidency.* Princeton, NJ: Princeton University Press.

U.S. Bureau of the Census. 1990. STF1A Table(s). Available at www.census.gov/cgi-bin/datamap/www.

Vinzant, J., and L. Crothers. 1994. Street-level leadership: Understanding community policing. *Criminal Justice Review* 19 (2): 189–211.

———. 1996. Street-level leadership: Rethinking the role of public servants in contemporary governance. *American Review of Public Administration* 26 (4): 457–475.

Volcker Commission. 1989. *Leadership for America: Rebuilding the public service.* Report of the national commission on the public service. Washington, DC: U.S. Government Printing Office, for the Committee on Post Office and Civil Service, U.S. House of Representatives.

Vroom, V., and A. Jago. 1988. *The new leadership: Managing participation in organizations.* Englewood Cliffs, NJ: Prentice Hall.

Vroom, V., and P. Yetton. 1973. *Leadership and decision making.* Pittsburgh: University of Pittsburgh Press.

Waldo, D. 1981. *The Enterprise of Public Administration.* Novato, CA: Chandler and Sharp Publishers.

Wamsley, G., R. Bacher, C. Goodsell, P. Kronenberg, J. Rohr, C. Stivers, O. White, and J. Wolf. 1990. *Refounding public administration.* Newbury Park, CA: Sage Publications.

Weakland, J., and L. Jordan. 1992. Working briefly with reluctant clients: Child protective services as an example. *Journal of Family Therapy* 14: 231–254.

Weber, M. 1946. In *From Max Weber: Essays in sociology,* translated and edited by H. Gerth & C. Mills, 1958. New York, NY: Oxford University Press.

Weimann, G. 1982. Dealing with bureaucracy: The effectiveness of different persuasive appeals. *Social Psychology Quarterly* 45: 136–144.

Weinbach, R. 1984. Implementing change: Insights and strategies for the supervisor. *Social Work* 29: 282–286.

West, C. 1996. Ethnography and orthography. *Journal of Contemporary Sociology* 25: 327–52.

Wilson, W. 1887. The study of administration. In *Classics of public administration*, 2nd ed., edited by J. Shafritz and A. Hyde (1987): 10–25. Chicago, IL: The Dorsey Press.

Worden, R. 1989. Situational and attitudinal explanations of police behavior: A theoretical reappraisal and empirical assessment. *Law and Society Review* 23 (4): 667–711.

Yukl, G. 1994. *Leadership in organizations*, 3rd ed. Englewood Cliffs: Prentice-Hall.

Index

access, and participant observation, 24–25
administrative conservatorship, 51
administrative procedure, and street-level leadership, 98–101
agencies. *See* public organizations
Arizona Department of Economic Security, 29, 168–69
assumptions, core, 6–9

Barth, T., 38
Bass, B., 81
behavioral theory of leadership, 77–79
Bennis, W., 75
Blanchard, K., 80–81, 103
Bohannon, W., 75
Brieland, D., 62
bureaucratic discretion. *See* discretion
bureaucratic model of public service, 54–56
Burns, James MacGregor, 86–88

clients, as environmental variable, 13
Collins, P., 65
community
    as environmental variable, 14–15
    policing, 62

complexity, and need for discretion, 44–47
Contingency Theory of Leadership, 80
courts, as environmental variable, 15
coworkers, as environmental variable, 13–14

Dahl, Robert, 83
decision-making environment. *See* environmental variables
decision-making theory. *See* problem-solver model of public service
Denhardt, R., 73
discretion
    concept of, 36–40
    evaluating exercise of, 47–48
    factors increasing need for, 42–47
    in general, 5–7, 20–21, 35–36, 141
    and leadership, 150–51
    and legitimacy, 7, 9, 36
    necessity of exercising, 40–42, 130
    within the leadership model, 91–94

Edley, C., 150

environmental variables
  complexity of interactions,
    17–19
  overview, 11–17
ethics, and participant observation, 25–26
evaluation of street-level public
  servants, xvii, 73, 156–58

failure of leadership on the street
  failure of leadership style, 132–
    33
  failure of legitimacy, 133–34
  failure of result, 131–32
  overview, 130–31
  uncertainty, 134–36
Fiedler, F., 80
Friedrich, C., 84
frontline workers. *See* street-level
  public servants

Gardner, J., 156
Geertz, C., 49
Giddens, A., 20
Glidewell, J., 23
Goldstein, H., 61
Goodnow, Frank, 54–55
Goodsell, C., 64–65
governance
  implementing leadership model
    within, 159–61
  implications of leadership model
    for, 149–52
  role of street-level public ser-
    vants, 19
government, opinions about, and
  discretion, 43, 146, 160
Green, C., 61
grounded theory, 20–21
Guyot, D., 62

Hargrove, Erwin, 23
Harmon, M., 44
Hart, R., 160

Hawthorne effect, and participant
  observation, 26–28
Hershey, P., 80–81, 103
Hopps, J., 65
Huntsville, Alabama, Police Depart-
  ment, 29, 165–67

Illinois Department of Children
  and Family Services, 29, 167–68

Jackman, R., 48, 50, 105

Kaplan, A., 142–43
Kass, H., 50–51, 93
Kearney, R., 59
Keller, L., 61
Kernell, S., 160
Kirkpatrick, S. A., 75
Kirlin, J., 143
Kurasawa, Akira, 48

language
  of street-level leadership, 73,
    146, 149
  theoretical significance of,
    143–44
Lasswell, H., 86
law, as environmental variable, 15
leadership
  behavioral theory of, 77–79
  concept of, 5–6, 72–73
  and power, 83–89
  public organizations, 148–49
  situational theories of, 79–83
  trait theory of, 74–77
  transformational theory of,
    88–89
  See also discretion
leadership model
  advantages of, 72–74, 141–42
  evolution of, 23–24
  governance, implications for,
    149–52
  overview, 5–6

public organizations, implications for, 148–49
specified, 91–94
street-level public servants, applied to. *See* leadership on the street
street-level public servants, implications for, 144–48
theory and practice, 142–44
leadership on the street
administrative procedure, 98–101
failure of, 130–36
in general, 89–90, 97–98
governance, implementing within, 159–61
limitations, 161–63
public organizations, implementing within, 154–59
situational, 101–12
situational and transformational combined, 122–30
street-level public servants, implementing among, 152–54
transformational, 112–22
legitimacy
analyzed in street actions, 104–5, 108–9, 117–18
concept of, 48–50
and discretion, 6, 7, 50–51
and failure of leadership on the street, 133–34
and power, 84–88
in public administration, 50–52
and street-level public servants, 51–54
See also discretion, and legitimacy
Linders, S., 57
line-level workers. *See* street-level public servants
Lipsky, Michael, 9, 12, 40–42, 57, 60–61, 92
Locke, E.A., 75
Lukes, Steven, 84

management approaches, and discretion, 42–43
Mayer, R., 44
media, as environmental variable, 15–16
methodology
evolution of study, 21–24
overview, 19–21
participant observation. *See* participant observation
subjects of study, 28–31, 165–69
Mills, C., 75
models, existing
assessment of, 66–67
bureaucratic, 54–56
organizational culture, 22–23
overview, 4–5, 54
policy implementation, 56–58
political actor, 64–66
power, 58–59
problem-solver, 61–64
professionalism, 59–61
models, leadership. *See* leadership model
Morgan, D., 49–51, 93
Morrow, W., 37
Mosher, F., 59
Muir, W., 58

Nakamura, R., 57
Newland, C., 60

organizational culture models, 22–23
Ott, J.S., 84

participant observation
described, 20–21
weaknesses, 8–9, 24–28
Peters, L., 57
phronesis, 51
police action
failure of street leadership, analysis, 135–36

police action (*continued*)
  failure of street leadership,
    examples, 132–33, 134–35
  general examples, x–xii, 1–2,
    52–53, 95–97, 98–100
  general examples, analysis, xiv–
    xvi, 17–19, 53
  situational and transforma-
    tional leadership combined,
    analysis, 126–27, 129–30
  situational and transforma-
    tional leadership combined,
    examples, 126, 127–29
  situational leadership, analysis,
    107–9, 110
  situational leadership, exam-
    ples, 107, 109–10
  transformational leadership,
    analysis, 114–16
  transformational leadership,
    examples, 112–14
policy implementation model of
  public service, 56–58
political actor model of public
  service, 64–66
power
  concept of, 83–84
  and legitimacy, 84–88
  model of public service, 58–59
  wielders, distinguished from
    leaders, 86–87
practice and theory, 3, 142–44
Pressman, J., 56–57
problems, wicked, 44–46, 162
problem-solver model of public
  service, 61–64
professionalism model of public
  service, 59–61
public administration, and legitimacy, 50–52
public organizations
  as environmental variable,
    12–13, 16
  implementing leadership model
    within, 154–59
  implications of leadership
    model, 148–49

public servants, street-level. *See*
  street-level public servants

rulers, distinguished from leaders,
  87
Russell, B., 83, 86

Sayre, W., 37
Schattschneider, E. E., 163
Shafritz, J., 48
Shinha, C., 59
situational leadership
  combined with transforma-
    tional leadership on the street,
    122–30
  on the street, 101–12
  theories, 79–83
situational variables, as environmental variable, 16
social-service worker actions
  failure of street leadership,
    examples, 133–34
  general examples, xii–xiv, 32–35,
    39–40, 45–46, 68–71, 85–86,
    137–40
  general examples, analysis, xvi–
    xvii, 35–36, 40, 46, 47–48, 55,
    63, 65–66, 93–94
  situational and transforma-
    tional leadership combined,
    analysis, 122–23, 125–26
  situational and transforma-
    tional leadership combined,
    examples, 122, 123–25
  situational leadership, analysis,
    103–5, 106–7, 111–12
  situational leadership, exam-
    ples, 101–3, 105–6, 110–11
  transformational leadership,
    analysis, 117–18, 119–20, 122
  transformational leadership,
    examples, 116–17, 118–19,
    120–22
Spicer, M., 65
Spokane County, Washington,
  Sheriff's Department, 29, 166–67

stewardship, 51

Stogdill, R., 72

street-level leadership. *See* leadership on the street

street-level public servants
core assumptions about, 6–8
difficulty of work, ix, 3–4
and discretion. *See* discretion
environment of. *See* environmental variables
evaluation of, xvii, 73, 156–58
implementing leadership model among, 152–54
implications of leadership model, 144–48
and leadership. *See* leadership; leadership on the street
models of. *See* models
need for a model, xvii–xviii
role defined, 9–10, 12
training of, 155–56

supervisors, as environmental variable, 16–17

Terry, L., 50–52, 65, 93

theory and practice, 3, 142–44

Thompson, R., 143

Total Quality Management, 43

training of street-level public servants, 155–56

trait theory of leadership, 74–77

transformational leadership
combined with situational leadership on the street, 122–30
on the street, 112–22
theory, 88–89

Tri-Dimensional Leadership Effectiveness Model, 80–81

Tullis, J., 160

Volcker Commission Report, 143, 149

Vroom-Yetton Contingency Model of Leadership, 80

Waldo, Dwight, 150

Wamsley, G., 61

Weber, M., 55

wicked problems, 44–46, 162

Wildavsky, A., 56–57

Wilson, Woodrow, 54–55

worker-centered approach, 8–9